History, evolution, and
the concept of culture

Alexander Lesser on a field trip to the Kiowa in Anadarko, Oklahoma, during the summer of 1935. The photograph was taken by one of his students. (Photograph by courtesy of Virginia Hirst Lesser.)

History, evolution, and the concept of culture

Selected papers by Alexander Lesser

Edited with introductions by
SIDNEY W. MINTZ
Department of Anthropology, The Johns Hopkins University

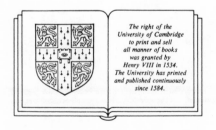

The right of the
University of Cambridge
to print and sell
all manner of books
was granted by
Henry VIII in 1534.
The University has printed
and published continuously
since 1584.

CAMBRIDGE UNIVERSITY PRESS
Cambridge
London   New York   New Rochelle
Melbourne   Sydney

Published by the Press Syndicate of the University of Cambridge
The Pitt Building, Trumpington Street, Cambridge CB2 1RP
32 East 57th Street, New York, NY 10022, USA
10 Stamford Road, Oakleigh, Melbourne 3166, Australia

First published 1985

Printed in the United States of America

Library of Congress Cataloging in Publication Data
Lesser, Alexander, 1902–1982
History, evolution, and the concept of culture.
Bibliography: p.
Includes index.
1. Ethnology – Addresses, essays, lectures.
2. Culture – Addresses, essays, lectures. 3. Social
evolution – Addresses, essays, lectures. I. Mintz,
Sidney Wilfred, 1922– . II. Title.
GN304.L47 1985 306 84–12732
ISBN 0 521 25860 X

Contents

Preface

Two years before his death, Alexander Lesser asked me to assist him in the preparation of a volume of his collected papers. I acceded immediately to his request, which greatly honored me. As a college sophomore, I had been Lesser's student in my first (and only) undergraduate course in anthropology. Though I had not the slightest idea of it at the time (1939), Lesser was then at the very height of his intellectual powers. For my efforts in his course, I received what I realize now to have been a generous "C." (Years later, when I was introducing Lesser to a Yale audience and mentioned the grade he had given me, he confessed to the audience that he had taken his first course in anthropology with Franz Boas, and that Boas had given him a "C"!) In spite of my mediocre performance, my esteem for Lesser was from the start considerable, even though I hardly knew why.

When I began to teach anthropology myself more than a decade later, I was impelled to recall what it had been about Lesser's presence in the classroom that had affected me. In spite of my callowness – the adolescent fear that a show of interest in what an older person thinks will be interpreted by one's peers as a sign of weakness, sycophancy, or naïveté – I remembered both liking and admiring the way Lesser acted. The reason why, reflection showed me, was quite simple: Lesser took himself and his subject seriously. He thought what he did mattered. He was serious about the importance of anthropology, serious about teaching it, and serious about his students. As I reflected further, I realized that many of my teachers had thought that teaching – and learning – were important to their society, as well as to their self-images. They derived much of their self-respect from the classroom. They thought that it was not only as good a place, but also as important a place as a bank, a barracks, an assembly line, a playing field, or a board room. I should perhaps stress that their feelings plainly did not depend upon their success in the classroom – for by no means were all successful. But whether they succeeded or failed as teachers, the classroom was where many of them felt they earned the right to practice their profession.

Lesser was that sort of teacher: He believed that what he *did* embodied who he *was*; and he believed that it was important to American society, and to himself, that he do it as well as he could. He thought anthropology could contribute toward making a better world by making us humans more aware of ourselves and of the forces – particularly the cultural forces – that affected us. Anthropologists, he believed, had an obligation to work at revealing those forces, in the classroom and out.

Anthropology and teaching have moved on since 1939, not altogether for the better. But I now realize that my own feelings about the aims of both anthropology and teaching derived in some measure from those conveyed to me by my teacher. Though I recognized the basis for my admiration only dimly at the time, Lesser's influence made its impression silently, even imperceptibly, upon my own sense of vocation. In recognition of that influence, I feel privileged to have been able to work with him during his final years in fashioning this book.

Although many of his students will think of Lesser first as a teacher, his lasting effect on anthropology flows even more from what he thought and wrote than from what he taught. Yet he was never prolific. His own bibliography of his writings lists but twenty-two items if we omit reprints, summaries of his work by other authors, his editorials in *The American Indian*, and a few brief reviews and specialized contributions. The list includes one monograph, *The Pawnee Ghost Dance Hand Game* (1933; reissued in 1978) and his unpublished doctoral dissertation. The remaining twenty essays can be classified roughly by subject as follows: religion, two; kinship, four; linguistics, one; race, one; Franz Boas, two; anthropology and modern life, four; and theory, six. Since Douglas Parks of Mary College is preparing a volume of Lesser's work in linguistics, and Raymond De Mallie of Indiana University (Bloomington) is doing the same with his work on kinship, there was no need to deal here with his achievements in those fields. The ten papers selected for this volume include one on religion, one on Boas, three on anthropology and modern life (one never before published), four of the six theory articles, and the foreword to the 1978 edition of his monograph on the Ghost Dance.

The collection represents a working accord between Lesser and myself. He and I consulted by mail and by telephone on many occasions concerning the essays to be reprinted, and readers of early outlines of the manuscript made suggestions as well. Lesser was particularly interested in the republication of his essays on evolution. It was his peculiar modesty, I think, that led him to recognize only at the end of his life how much ahead of their time were his early papers in anthropological theory. We aimed at striking a balance that would represent his range of competence without tilting sharply toward the heavily technical and ethnographic end of the spectrum. But Lesser's untimely death, only shortly before the cheering news reached me that Cambridge University Press had accepted the manuscript, left me to make some of the final decisions about what was to be included, and those very familiar with his work may find favorite articles missing. The final, rather arbitrary, grouping of the articles into four sections is also my responsibility.

The corpus of Lesser's writings is modest compared to that of many of his contemporaries and successors. But his work is rich in critical insight and originality, and his technical papers are typified by the detailed and rigorous treatment of the trained ethnographer. His sallies into matters of public policy and his dedication to making anthropology useful to society repeatedly revealed his intellectual youthfulness and lack of pretense.

On one occasion, I was privileged to invite him to give an inaugural lecture marking the establishment of the Department of Anthropology at Johns Hopkins University. He gave a vigorous and exciting lecture, then carried on a lively discussion with the faculty and students. Toward midnight, I asked him whether he was ready to go to sleep. "You know," he said, "if none of you were here, I could lie down on that couch and fall asleep in a minute. But as long as people want to talk anthropology, I do, too." Such was Alexander Lesser's unforgettable spirit.

In preparing the manuscript I was helped by many friends and associates. Virginia Hirst Lesser (Mrs. Alexander Lesser) and Ann Margetson (the daughter of Alexander Lesser and the late Gene Weltfish) provided ideas. Tom Biolsi, Sol Miller, Doug Parks, and Joan Vincent supplied useful information of all kinds. Kenneth Bilby, John V. Murra, Kathleen S. Ryan, Rebecca Scott, and particularly William C. Sturtevant gave me valuable substantive and editorial criticism. At an early stage, Ray Fogelson and David and Kathrine S. French made trenchant critical readings. Later Ashraf Ghani and Joan Vincent did the same. Ashraf Ghani made especially useful specific suggestions for improving the general Introduction and the Introduction to Part I. Ray DeMallie and Doug Parks were very helpful in locating suitable materials for the dust jacket design. Elise LeCompte gave me indispensable assistance from the inception of the project almost until its conclusion. Deborah Caro showed both care and good sense in preparing the index. To the editorial staff of the Cambridge University Press I have several debts: to Sue Allen-Mills, in particular, for her faith in this project; and to Sue Comfort, Sue Potter, and Linda Spencer, for their valuable help with the manuscript along the way.

Sidney W. Mintz

Introduction

The essays of Alexander Lesser are critical documents in the history of American anthropology. In his teaching and research, Lesser specialized in the study of North American Indians, above all the cultures of those groups referred to in the anthropological literature as "Plains Indians." In addition, Lesser devoted many years of his professional life to the cause of American Indians. By combining teaching, research, and policy activity on, for, and with American Indians during the course of his career, he distinguished himself among the anthropologists of his generation.

Lesser mentions John Dewey and Alexander Goldenweiser as among the major figures in his intellectual development. But it was Franz Boas who had the most profound effect. In the 1920s, Lesser was one of the "second wave" of Boas students at Columbia University that also included George Herzog, Melville Jacobs, and Gene Weltfish (to whom Lesser was married for many years). Boas was then at the height of a career that embodied one of the most powerful (and, in the United States, one of the most disturbing) traditions in the whole history of social science, a tradition that Lesser and many others have helped to reveal and recall. (See, for instance, American Anthropological Association 1943, Goldschmidt 1949, Stocking 1974, Lesser 1968a, and Part I of this volume.)

Lesser's intellectual accomplishments bespeak Boas's influence in manifold ways. Yet, as the essays reprinted in this volume attest, he went beyond "Boasianism." The further development of Boas's anthropology was hampered by the kinds of general – one might almost say philosophical – stands he was compelled to take, given the political and social climate of his adopted homeland, the United States. Lesser's ability to break away from the constraints that bound his teacher marked his distinctive contribution to anthropology. His scholarship reveals not only how he labored to remain loyal to the viewpoint of his teacher, but also the brilliance of his insight when he succeeded in going further in certain important theoretical directions than Boas was prepared to go.

1

Any regrouping of essays that have been chosen from different periods of an individual's intellectual development is by definition arbitrary and does some violence to the chronological continuity of theoretical effort. The arrangement of this volume is no exception. The articles have been grouped into four sections, each with an introduction aimed at helping the reader appreciate Lesser's contribution in four distinguishable domains of anthropology. The first section, "Boasian anthropology," suggests both what Lesser learned from Boas and how he went beyond him. The second section, "Theory and method," is separable from the third, "Evolution," only by a kind of Alexandrine decision, for both sections deal with theory, and the essays in "Theory and method" are also related to Lesser's evolutionary perspective. The essays in the last section, "Anthropology and modern life," express Lesser's lifelong interest in North American Indians as well as his concern about the applicability of anthropology to human needs.

There is an unusual intellectual continuity and consistency in Lesser's writings, from his first published paper to the last. "Caddoan kinship systems," published in 1979, was based on materials gathered half a century earlier, but it is no less focused, and reveals no significantly different theoretical stance, than the first essay he wrote on Caddoan groups (1929a). There was, however, a long period during which Lesser published very little. The fit of his periods of greater productivity with world events is clear, for his scholarly work is in effect concentrated in two periods: the first the years just after he finished his dissertation in 1929; the second near the end of his career.

The theoretical high point of Lesser's work falls in the years 1933–39. Before the war, he taught at Columbia University, Brooklyn College, and elsewhere, counting among his students such leaders of anthropology as Joseph Greenberg, Oscar Lewis, and Charles Wagley. Many of the students who accompanied him on the Kiowa Field Training Expedition in 1935, including William Bascom, Donald Collier, and Weston La Barre, also eventually had an important influence on American anthropology. Some of them, like Bernard Mishkin and Jane Richardson Hanks, wrote dissertations based on the experience. Lesser's article and monograph on the Ghost Dance (see Chapters 8 and 9) appeared in 1933, and "Functionalism in social anthropology" (Chapter 3) in 1935. These three works, though very different in substance, are related through Lesser's concern with history as a tool for the explanation of social and cultural change. Two of his finest papers, on procedures and directives in anthropological research (Chapters 2 and 4), were published in 1939, and show Lesser actively doubting the received wisdom of the whole profession. His best-known paper on evolution (Chapter 5), almost a taboo topic at the time, was presented at a professional meeting the same year (though it was not published until 1952).

Like many others of the time, Lesser's career was deeply affected by the Second World War. The war period interrupted his teaching and research for longer than he had expected. In 1943, he began his government service in the Office of the Coordinator for Interamerican Affairs. He was transferred the following year to the Office of Strategic Services (OSS). In 1946, when the OSS closed up shop, he was awarded a Certificate of Merit. He then became a research analyst with the Latin America Branch of the U.S. State Department's Office of Research Intelligence, where he remained until 1947. Because he was unable to get a teaching post, from government service Lesser went to the Association on American Indian Affairs, where he served as Executive Director for eight years, until 1955. During the period from 1947 to 1955 he published numerous articles and (in his role as editor of *The American Indian*) editorials dealing with policy matters concerning American Indians, but wrote little of a theoretical nature. There is no doubt that more of Lesser's work would have been published eventually, had it not been for the war years and for his lengthy stay at the Association while he was unable to obtain a teaching position.

It was only in 1956, after a hiatus of thirteen years, that Lesser was able to return to teaching, first at Brandeis University and thereafter at Hofstra. His second period of scholarly productivity came after he had returned to full-time teaching. In 1961, he published an important paper on the position of the American Indian (Chapter 7) and a perceptive essay on social fields (Chapter 6). He contributed a new foreword (Chapter 9) to the paperback edition of *The Pawnee Ghost Dance Hand Game* in 1978, and in 1981 prepared his lengthy essay on Franz Boas (Chapter 1) for publication. Chapter 10 is a previously unpublished paper he delivered as a Distinguished Lecture at Calgary University in 1974.

Lesser's contributions toward a unified social science and an anthropology with policy implications are as important as his contributions to descriptive ethnography and "pure science." His stress upon the interrelatedness and orderliness of social phenomena, his belief in a genuinely scientific anthropology, his insistence on an anthropology that could produce practical insights for solving human problems, his use of conceptual materials to enhance the explanatory value of field data – all allowed him to rise above ethnographic particularism and to shatter conventional notions of what cultural anthropology was thought to be half a century ago.

Lesser's admiration for Boas was matched by his own desire to make anthropology relevant to the solution of the everyday problems of ordinary people. His view of Boas as citizen-scientist clearly expressed his own feelings about the aims and worthwhileness of his discipline (see Chapter 1). Those who knew Lesser from his performances at scholarly meetings will remember his unusual ability to find the larger inconsistencies in "schools" of anthropological thought, address them from the floor, and expose them concisely. At the 1959 Annual Spring Meeting of the American Ethnological Society (AES), to note but one instance, he attacked the idea of the "intermediate society" so effectively that the architect of the concept asked him to contribute a piece to the proceedings (see Lesser 1959). The ideas in that short AES essay are represented in this collection in "Social fields and the evolution of society" (Chapter 6).

His ideas on war surface nowhere in this book, but in an essay *The New York Times* commissioned in 1968 (but never printed), Lesser underlined his conviction that war, like most massive contemporary problems, is a problem that must be addressed by the social sciences:

It is not atomic energy that is the terror of the atomic age, but the *social and political relationships* among peoples which threaten nuclear *war*. Atoms for peace rather than war is a problem of behavioral relationships, not of physics. All the fundamental problems of our time are problems of human relationships, not technology. . . . Peace is not even understood positively – it is for most, scientists and laymen alike, the absence of war. Most of the "peace" in the world, like the "peace" in the Near East, or the "Cold War" of the U.S. and the U.S.S.R., is merely an "armed truce," with fingers steadily fingering the "buttons" and the triggers.

What does social science *know* about war? In 1945, under the leadership of Gardner Murphy, American psychologists published a symposium on *Human Nature and Enduring Peace,* and the first principle to which all subscribed is: War can be avoided; war is not born in men; it is built into men. Anthropologists have shown that many cultures and societies have existed *without war* so that war and militarism are not inherent in the nature of human society. Psychology and anthropology concur that "instincts" are not involved in adult human behavior, and that aggression is not innate in man. The current crop of pseudo-science (by non-social scientists) trying to prove the opposite is rationalization of our national and international commitment to war as a normal feature of human political life. Even on an individual basis, aggression is patently not innate. . . . Obviously, we *assume* aggression is there in the baby – all babies – and got "sublimated" out of some. This is not science, but fairy tales.

In "War and the state" (1968b), Lesser carries his argument further, pointing out that armed conflict takes radically different forms in societies having different technical bases, different economies, and different sizes. He draws on his own extensive knowledge of Plains Indian warfare, and emphasizes the examination of reliable data on the fighting behavior of particular peoples. Though he criticizes "disembodied fantasies of theory," Lesser is not calling for an end to theory – far from it. Rather, he is insisting on the need to relate theory and facts, a need anthropologists clearly benefit from being reminded of at regular intervals. Moreover, he is arguing that anthropologists have something important to say about a subject matter they have usually ignored, leaving it to other scholars to settle.

It was because of his commitment to a holistic view of culture that was "functional" as well as "historical" that Lesser was as impatient with much of the so-called history of many American anthropologists as he was with much of the so-called functionalism of many British anthropologists. A functionalism that found no room for the effects of European conquest upon the indigenous institutions of the conquered peoples struck him as odd indeed – though his skepticism was shared by a surprisingly small number of his colleagues in the United States. And a historicism that counted in infinite detail the items of material culture in an indigenous society, in order to repeat the process with dozens of neighboring societies and then to attempt to reconstruct their "history" statistically, struck him as equally odd.

In melding so convincingly functionalism and historical method in his own work, Lesser avoided the sterility of both distributional studies and ahistorical functionalism. Only a few anthropologists of his time paid attention. A genuine functional historicity has only recently reemerged – at times with somewhat startling fanfare about pioneering this or that. Lesser was a prophet for his own profession. But prophets are always ahead of their time.

Part I

Boasian anthropology

Introduction to Part I

The two essays in this section are different in kind and were written at significantly different points in Lesser's career, yet they clearly belong together. The first, "Franz Boas and the modernization of anthropology," was delivered as a lecture at several universities in the 1970s, before it was prepared for publication. Its appearance in 1981 in a collection edited by Sydel Silverman followed by thirteen years another essay Lesser had written on Boas, for the *International Encyclopedia of the Social Sciences,* that documented Boas's scientific accomplishments (Lesser 1968a). The 1981 essay is concerned as much with Boas as a public and political figure as with his scientific position and achievements. In the ways that he interpreted Boas's work and his scientific stance, one can readily discern where Lesser learned many of his own habits of mind about the objectives of anthropology, if it is to be used in the service of humanity.

The second essay, "Research procedure and the laws of culture," was written in 1939, during the most productive period of Lesser's scholarly life. It belongs with the paper on Boas because it reveals to the reader the powerful intellectual stimuli (and one supposes, equally powerful constraints) that Lesser must have experienced as Boas's student. If viewed from the perspective of Lesser's theoretical development, however, it could just as well have been included in Part III.

From 1896 until 1936, when he retired, Franz Boas represented anthropology at Columbia University. Silverman (1981:2–3) has pointed out that Boas produced two generations of anthropologists during his lifetime, each of which in turn produced yet others influenced by the same fundamental ideas. For many American anthropologists, though emphatically not for all, Boas's views became almost synonymous with the discipline of anthropology.

In an essay that throws much light on Boas and his students, Eric Wolf has distinguished three stages in the intellectual history of American anthropology. The second stage, which he calls "the period of intermittent

9

Liberal Reform," dates from near the end of the last century to the Second World War and corresponds to the Boas era:

The assertion of a collectivity of common men against the anarchistic captains of industry was represented by Beard, Turner, Veblen, Commons, Dewey, Brandeis, and Holmes; in American anthropology, the reaction against Social Darwinism found its main spokesman in Franz Boas. His work in physical anthropology furnished some of the initial arguments against a racism linked to Social Darwinist arguments. In his historical particularism he validated a shift of interest away from the grand evolutionary schemes to concern with the panoply of particular cultures in their historically conditioned setting. If we relate these anthropological interests to the tenor of the times, we can say that the renewed interest in cultural plurality and relativity had two major functions. It called into question the moral and political monopoly of an elite which had justified its rule with the claim that their superior virtue was the outcome of the evolutionary process – it was their might which made their right. . . . For the intellectual prophets of the times the preeminent instruments for the achievement of this cooperative participation among new and diverse elements were to be scientific education and liberal reform achieved through social engineering. . . . The tool for discovery of the manifold educational processes – and hence also for a more adequate approach to the engineering of pluralistic education – was science, that is, anthropology. The faith in social engineering and in the possibility of a new educational pluralism also underwrote the action programs among American Indians, who by means of the new techniques were to become autonomous participants in a more pluralistic and tolerant America.

But . . . the anthropology of Liberal Reform did not address itself, in any substantive way, to the problem of power . . . only rarely – if at all – did anthropologists shift their scientific focus to the constraints impeding both human malleability and malleability in socialization from the outside. . . . The culture-and-personality schools of the 30's and 40's made a moral paradigm of each individual culture. They spoke of patterns, themes, world view, ethos, and values, but not of power. . . . Neither in the 19th century nor in the first half of the 20th century, therefore, did American anthropology as such come to grips with the phenomenon of power (Wolf 1969:5–7).

It is quite true that Boas did not pay close attention to the concept of power in his analyses, or use power as an explanatory device in his own research – in his work on non-Western societies, the issues of power and class are relatively neglected. But as Lesser's essay on Boas (Chapter 1) demonstrates, that he was nonetheless aware of power and its uses is clear from his outspokenness on many public issues, and from the consequences of some of his most unpopular stands, such as his opposition to American participation in the First World War.

By leaving unaddressed the possibility that class divisions might be found in all societies, Boas left room for the idea that, rather than being linked to the history of particular social institutions – property, law, forms of marriage, religious systems – class might instead constitute some universal natural attribute of human society. In his famous book on social classes, the economist and economic historian Joseph Schumpeter, a colleague of Boas's before the First World War, wrote that "neither historically nor ethnologically has its [class's] utter absence been demonstrated in even a single case" (Schumpeter 1955:112). Schumpeter cites Gumplowicz, Marx, Sombart, and Haddon in support of one or another part of his argument; yet he makes not a single mention of Boas, pro or con. But though Boas's position on this issue was unclear, his work was crucial to the views of other scholars, who saw in the concept of culture a powerful instrument for understanding both social status and social change. John Dewey was one of them. In the essay on human nature Lesser quotes near the end of Chapter 1, Dewey observes that "many of the obstacles to change which have been attributed to human nature are in fact due to the inertia of institutions and to the voluntary desire of powerful classes to maintain the existing status" (Dewey 1932:536). Even though Boas did not (to my knowledge) ever state such views so succinctly, the link between his position and Dewey's is clear.

What has doubtless been perceived as the more enduringly subversive idea within "Boasianism" is Boas's commitment to a *science* of humankind and what that implied for United States society as it was constituted during the first half of this century. In effect, Boas argued for an objective and value-free approach to the comparative study of all cultures, especially those of technically less advanced peoples. He was never prepared to assume that any differences in intellectual capacity or in moral worth obtained between one society or human group and any other. He created, largely by his own research, a physical anthropology that lent no support to preconceptions about the significance of physical differences between or among human groups. He argued eloquently and convincingly for the separation of race, a genetic concept, from language and culture, which are socially acquired and historically derived accompaniments to human group existence. Though his anthropology was concentrated on so-called primitive peoples, particularly American Indians, he carried out investigations (and supported his students' research) among European immigrants, Africans, Puerto Ricans, and Black Americans; in Melanesia and Polynesia; and on the Jesup Expedition to Siberia. His work was consistently initiated on the premise that culture is a distinctively human property that is shared equally by all human beings.

It is only in the light of what Wolf calls "the tenor of the times" that the implications of Boasian anthropology and its scientific contentions about human nature can be seen for what they were. During the period

1890–1920, the complete undoing of Reconstruction was being celebrated and a reign of terror against Black Americans was becoming institutionalized, vast masses of penniless and uneducated European immigrants were arriving in the United States, and the military elimination of American Indians as a political force looked at last to be fully assured. If we then add to this picture that Boas was a German-Jewish immigrant who lived in New York City, taught at Columbia University, and had many Jewish, foreign, and female students, we should not be surprised that he is reviled to this day, more than forty years after his death, by racists, sexists, anti-Semites, xenophobes, and chauvinists. And his achievements – that he was honored around the world for his scholarship, that his scientific integrity was never impugned by other scholars, that his reorganization of American anthropology affected the discipline nearly everywhere, and that he succeeded in finding support for his students in spite of his outspokenness on pressing public issues – are all the more cause for wonder.

In the first essay of Part I, Lesser seeks to situate Franz Boas, both as a scientific pioneer in anthropology and as a political figure of his time. But in the second, he undertakes a more difficult task: to establish Boas as a social evolutionist. Lesser seeks to document regularities or casual sequences in culture and offers a series of examples, some of regularly interdependent (or functional) relationships and others of patterned sequences (historical or diachronic regularities). He draws heavily on Boas's own work in his attempt to refute assertions that Boas had no interest in causation, in social (as opposed to biological) evolution, or in social and cultural regularities. Oddly enough – though he did not recognize it until others later made it clear – the more convincing portions of the argument are Lesser's. But some of his own originality is diminished by the way in which he argues, for though it is somewhat anticipatory to make the assertion here, Lesser is caught up in this essay by his desire to go beyond the anthropology of his teacher without appearing to differ with him.

If Boas was antievolutionary – as I believe him to have been – his antievolutionism was actually rooted in two quite different concerns. He was, of course, an organic (Darwinian) evolutionist. But his lack of enthusiasm for social or cultural evolutionary theory originated, I believe, not only in the state of anthropological theory at the turn of the century, but also in the strategic importance of the spurious evolutionism evident in American political and economic thought of the times.

Boas had little interest in broad causative generalities about humankind or its history, believing that many detailed ethnographic studies would have to be realized before any evolutionary principles at all could be formulated. He was, moreover, offended by any pseudo-evolutionism that likened human societies to steps, some higher and some lower, on a moral or intellectual ladder – views very common in American academic and business circles that were frequently used to justify what was popularly referred to as "the march of civilization" on absolutely no scientific grounds whatever. In *Aunt Polly's Story of Mankind,* satirist Donald Ogden Stewart portrays with charm and affection just such an evolutionist. Robert and Helen Lynd (1929:4–5) point out that Aunt Polly documents "the process of evolution as the ascent from the nasty amoeba to Uncle Frederick triumphantly standing at the top of the long and tortuous course in a Prince Albert with one gloved hand resting upon the First National Bank and the other upon the Presbyterian Church." It is sobering to discover how many Uncle Fredericks were in academic garb, rather than in Prince Alberts, in Boas's time.

Lesser seeks to show, however, that Boas was not hostile to generalizations. It is significant that the work he found most suitable for his purposes was an encyclopedia article (Boas 1930a), the very form of which compelled Boas to produce one of the very few essays in generalization to be found in his copious bibliography. For though it is indeed possible to discover in Boas a positive attitude toward the identification of sociocultural regularities in history and in society, he was also, as Lesser himself carefully points out in the 1981 essay (Chapter 1), dissatisfied with the eagerness of his listeners to apply and reformulate generalizations, and accordingly grew more and more unwilling to formulate such "rules" or "laws" of culture.

There is, of course, no necessary connection at all between evolutionism seriously interested in the causes and mechanisms of cultural change through time and evolutionism aimed at justifying existing power relations by scientifically unsupportable references to "natural selection" or "nature red in tooth and claw." But I suspect Boas feared that any compliance on his part with cultural "evolutionism" of any sort would have led him ineluctably into the camp of the "tooth and claw" theorists, whose methods (as well as motives) he found entirely unacceptable.

Lesser's attempt to rehabilitate Boas as an evolutionist therefore says more about Lesser's originality and imaginativeness as a pioneer of the new evolution than it does about Boas. Boas may not have objected to Lesser's view – Lesser quotes him on nearly every page – but one suspects that he could not have been very interested in this line of argument. What is more, one wonders whether Lesser would have been able to pitch the argument at all had he not had the encyclopedia article as a basis.

One is led to wonder what other scholars may have affected Lesser's interpretation of the ideas of his principal teacher and to what extent his own evolutionary conceptions, rather than flowing from Boas's teachings, represent other intellectual traditions. Elsewhere in his work Lesser mentions that he was much influenced by V. Gordon Childe, the Australian archaeologist of Europe and the Middle East who was himself much influenced by Marx. He also mentions favorably Henry James Sumner Maine, the great English student of comparative jurisprudence whose work has an evolutionary character, and he refers several times to the work of G. C. Wheeler on the indigenous peoples of Australia. Wheeler is perhaps best remembered in anthropology today as one of the triumvirate of Hobhouse, Wheeler, and Ginsberg, whose *Material Culture and Social Institutions of the Simpler Peoples* (1915) was a frankly social evolutionary early work. It seems probable, however, that Lesser, like most scholars, was only partially aware of his own intellectual origins. All the more remarkable, then, to find so thoughtful an evolutionary position espoused in 1939, by an American anthropologist and a "Boasian" at that.

1 Franz Boas and the modernization of anthropology

In retrospect, Franz Boas was the builder and architect of modern anthropology.[1] This has come to be a general consensus, despite certain controversies. I propose to focus on four themes in his life and work:

1. The way in which Boas filled the role of architect of modern anthropology.
2. What Boas brought with him into anthropology that was the effective factor of factors in modernizing it.
3. How Boas, anthropologist and scientist, was a *citizen-scientist* all his life, whose ethics and ideals for the study of man were far-reaching, humane, and still hold true in our own day.
4. How Boas, far from being antitheory, was himself *the* great theorist of modern anthropology, who established the core of anthropological theory on which the science is based.

Modern anthropology begins with Franz Boas. It begins in the scientific skepticism with which he examined the traditional orthodoxies of the study of man, exposing and rejecting the false and unproven, calling for a return to empirical observation, establishing the truth of elementary fundamentals, opening new pathways and creating new methods. It begins in Boas' ways of thinking about man and his history, in his use of rigorous scientific requirements for data and for proof, in his rejection of old myths, old stereotypes, old emotionally charged assumptions.

Boas' contribution to the transformation of anthropology was therefore not a simple, single event, a formal statement of principles, or a generalized theory at a certain point of time. Boas worked from problem to problem, consolidating the truth gained and asking the next question. The framework and principles of the modern subject matter are emergents from this ongoing process, in part the residue of truth left after traditional materials and ideas were reevaluated, in part the positive discovery of empirical principles by fresh and original observation.

This essay was originally published as "Franz Boas and the modernization of anthropology," by Alexander Lesser, in Sydel Silverman, ed., *Totems and Teachers*, pp. 3–31. © 1981 Columbia University Press. Reproduced by permission.

Boas was aware of this critical character of his method from his early professional years. In 1907, responding at Columbia to a Festschrift which was given him on the twenty-fifth anniversary of his Ph.D., he described himself as "one whose work rests essentially in an unfeeling criticism of his own work and that of others" (Boas 1907:646). He wrote a defense of the cephalic index (head form) and its traditional importance as a hereditary trait only a few years before his own research proved it was not strictly genetically determined but was affected significantly by environmental change (Boas 1899, 1911a). He condemned his early Kwakiutl and other Northwest Coast research as questionable, superseded by later work (Boas 1897, 1901). He came to "disparage his early work on the Kwakiutl language," pointing out its shortcomings (Boas 1930b:ix, cited in Codere 1966:xiv). He was continually self-critical. "Flawless perfection, then, must not be sought in Boas," as Lowie (1944b:64) has put it.

But in the end he restructured anthropology and its branches, leading physical anthropology from taxonomical race classification into human biology, breaking through the limitations of traditional philology into the problems of modern linguistics and cognitive anthropology, establishing the modern anthropological meaning and study of human culture.

Along his way, as Boas worked at problems in all fields of anthropology, he came to discoveries and understanding which, through his writing and teaching, became the convictions and effected the consensus from which the modern science of anthropology was born. Many of his writings were summations of plateaus of understanding he had reached in one area of anthropology or another. *The Mind of Primitive Man* in 1911 was his first great general consolidation in book form, a seminal book in modern social thought for technical readers and the lay public alike. In it, Boas reorganized and integrated studies of 1894 to 1911 into closely argued theses which became baselines of anthropology thereafter and fundamental conceptions in social science and social philosophy.

The book provided general anthropology and its separable branches – physical anthropology, linguistics, ethnology – with a structural framework. Establishing the relative autonomy of cultural phenomena, it gave to the concept of culture its modern meaning and usage. Boas proved that cultures are diverse historical developments, each the outcome of a prior history in which many factors and events, cultural and noncultural, have played a part. He made the plurality of cultures fundamental to the study of man (see Stocking 1968:203). He showed how languages, both semantically and morphologically, are each a context of perception that affects human thought and action. Analogously, he showed how cultural environments, especially as contexts of traditional materials, shape and structure human behavior – actions and reactions – in each generation. In so doing he ended the traditional ambiguity in the term *culture* understood interchangeably as both humanistic and behavioral – an ambiguity perpetuated by endless quoting of Tylor's "culture *or* civilization" – and started the modern era of the concept of *cultures,* viewed as contexts of learned human behavior.

A much earlier paper shows that the same essential conception was in his mind more than twenty years before. In "The Aims of Ethnology" (written in 1888), Boas stated, "The data of ethnology prove that not only our language, but also our emotions are the result of the form of our social life and of the history of the people to whom we belong" (Boas 1940a:636). The concept of social heritage was basic to Boas' thinking all his life.

Several of the theses of the book *The Mind of Primitive Man,* taken together, establish the relative autonomy of cultural phenomena, showing that there are *no independent variables* on which the cultural is dependent. First, establishing that race (physical type), language, and culture have relatively independent histories and are not interchangeable terms in classifying man, Boas showed that inner inborn traits ("race" or heredity) are not causal determinants of similarities or differences of cultures. Second, showing that geographical or natural environments are not neatly correlated with cultures as adaptations but always involve preexisting cultures, Boas proved that outer environmental conditions are not *the* causal determinants of similarities or differences of cultures. Finally, establishing that ideas of *orthogenetic* cultural evolution do not fit the facts of actual cultural sequences and history, Boas showed that no necessary predetermining process of change makes similarities or differences of cultures expressions of unfolding stages of development. These theses became principles of modern anthropology.

It is, I think, important to understand what it was in Boas' training and point of view that led him into the critical reconstruction of anthropology that he accomplished. This is especially important because of further implications for the understanding of Boas' thinking on theory and scientific method. It has been widely held that it was Boas' training in physics and mathematics that was responsible for his scientific reconstruction of the field of anthropology, which was largely preprofessional and somewhat amateurish at the time. Actually, I am convinced that it was an entirely different phase of his education and scientific experience that led to his future work, and I believe he tried to make that clear in his own statements.

Central to Boas' education in science and scientific thinking was the study of natural history, in which he indulged that "intense interest in nature" that he later recalled as characteristic of his youth (Boas 1938a:201–4). Boas attended the Froebel kindergarten in Minden founded and taught by his mother, which provided special nature studies. This experience was unusual for Boas' time, for kindergartens were rare then. Periods of recuperation after illness, spent in the countryside of Clus or at the seaside at Helgoland, acquainted him with the plant life of the woods and the wealth of animals and plants of the sea. He collected his own herbarium and for years "treasured" – his own word – the sea life specimens he gathered at Helgoland. He had a mineral collection and began to study mineralogy early in his Gymnasium years. In mid-Gymnasium he studied some zoology (including study on his own of the comparative bone structure of geese, ducks, and hares); astronomy and geology; more botany – physiology, plant anatomy, and the geographical distribution of plants. His interest in this last subject almost stifled other hobbies, but the study of cryptograms (plants such as ferns, moss, and algae, which reproduce by spores), begun in his own early herbarium collecting, became with a special teacher a subject which fascinated him ever after.

In his later Gymnasium years, drawn to all the natural sciences, he studied plant anatomy and physiology, used microscope in plant study and in work on crystal forms and systems in mineralogy, and made his own map of the distribution of plants in the Minden region. In the universities, the special professors he sought included two biologists (one also a marine biologist), a botanist, and two mineralogists (one also a geologist). He found his studies of plant distributions among his most exciting work, and was elated when, by mid-Gymnasium years – for the most part through study on his own – he could follow fairly well "the evolution of the animal and plant world" and "its transient geographical distribution" (APS, 1).

Natural history with its empirical approach involved Boas in observation, description, comparison and classification, inductive generalization, and *an acceptance of the external world* which became a habit of thinking for Boas. In attempting to understand Boas and what he contributed to modern thought, his statements about his "intellectual interest" in physics and mathematics have been overemphasized, while other statements about his "intensive emotional interest in the phenomena of the world" – along with his long concentration on natural history studies – have been given too little attention. Boas' background before he became an anthropologist included physics and mathematics as well as geography as part of his intellectual training. But to understand what he made of anthropology it is far more important to know that he came to the study of man as a naturalist, as a student of natural history, and tried to understand man and peoples as part of the natural phenomena of the world.

Among anthropologists, Marian W. Smith is virtually alone in emphasizing this mode of understanding Boas. In a paper on Boas' approach to field method, Smith draws a sharp contrast between Boas' "natural history approach to the social sciences" and the "social philosophy approach of British social anthropology," and she shows that the contrast affected both the methods and content of fieldwork done by the two schools (Smith 1959:46).[2] The American approach includes all of culture, considers data inviolable, and seeks in data only generalizations or theories that can be reached inductively. The British school, in contrast, begins with assumptions and theories and uses field data and the field situation to test hypotheses that have been deductively derived.

Marian Smith's paper limits the scope of her interpretations, but one suspects from some of her comments that she would have gone on to a conception of Boas and his thinking similar to my own. For example, she says:

Boas, more than any other person, first brought the very mind of man into the natural world. . . . Conceptualization and philosophy no longer breathed a finer air. They could be studied by the same techniques and approaches, by the same attitudes as other human characteristics and consequently lost much of their aura of revealed truth (Smith 1959:46).

Smith's paper had a singular impact on some anthropologists. For example, Kroeber, in his discussion of "Boas: The Man," had emphasized the mathematical and physical character of Boas' education, training, and lifelong modes of thought (Kroeber 1943:5–7). Even earlier, in 1935, in a famous exchange with Boas on history, Kroeber had written:

To begin with, it is of indubitable significance that Boas' educational training was in the physical laboratory sciences, in physics in fact. This led him into psychophysics and physical geography. His doctoral dissertation was on the color of sea water. This in turn led to a one-man, two-year geographical expedition to Baffinland, which brought with it intimate contacts with natives. The result was *The Central Eskimo* and a career of anthropology since. From physics Boas brought into anthropology a sense of definiteness of problem, of exact rigor of method, and of highly critical objectivity. These qualities have remained with him unimpaired, and his imparting them to anthropology remains his fundamental and unshakeable contribution to our discipline (Kroeber 1935:539–40).

This attitude of Kroeber's is completely contrary to Boas' own explanation of his manner of thinking. In a paper called "The Study of Geography," in 1887, Boas specifically contrasts the methods of physics with the methods of history (Boas 1940a:639–47). He uses "physics" and "history" as conceptual terms for two general types of approaches, the former seeking laws and subordinating particular events to abstract gen-

eralizations, the latter seeking the thorough understanding of phenomena
– even individual events – and making laws or generalizations merely
instrumental to that end. Boas identifies himself with the historical approach, temperamentally, in interests, and in methods, and he is unsym-
pathetic to that of physics.

In contrast to his earlier statements, Kroeber wrote in his 1959 preface
to *The Anthropology of Franz Boas,* the volume which contains Marian
Smith's paper, that "natural scientists have never questioned the status
of Boas and the importance of his massive contribution," that Boas' anthropological activity at first stemmed largely from both natural history
and humanist interests, and that Boas dealt so extensively with non-European and nonclassical languages because they are a part of the total
world of nature. "Given the combination of Boas' natural science adhe-
sion and his predilection for human materials, it was almost inevitable
that he should concern himself with culture, for culture, including its
semiautonomous province of language, is precisely the phenomenal regularities of human behavior" (Kroeber 1959:vi). This is fundamentally
different from Kroeber's statements of a few years earlier.

Solon Kimball has made a special point of relating the "natural history"
approach to anthropology itself. In a paper presented at an American
Anthropological Association meeting some years ago, he offered the thesis that anthropology had developed historically from the approach of
natural history, while sociology had developed from the approach of physics and the formal deductive sciences. Kimball had consistently taken the
position – especially in studies of the relation of anthropology to methods
and principles of modern education – that anthropology is rooted in the
method of natural history (as exemplified by Darwin) and involved "inductive empiricism based upon methods of classification and interdepen-
dencies of components" (Kimball, personal communication).

Empirical methods to Boas meant firsthand experience where data were
lacking. It meant an end to brilliantly constructed speculations as a substitute for observation. In ethnology, of course, this meant fieldwork, and
Boas' own work on the Eskimos is generally recognized as one early
example which stimulated the development of fieldwork as the basis of
ethnology and cultural anthropology. In discussions of the historical development of ethnology, attention is often drawn (as by Evans-Pritchard)
to the Torres Straits Expedition of the English, in which W. H. R. Rivers
and A. C. Haddon participated. Yet much of the work of that expedition
was peripheral to ethnology, as, for example, the effort of Rivers to settle
psychological questions of the sensibilities of indigenous peoples. Somewhat overlooked in this historical view are the monumental field re-

searches of the Jesup North Pacific Expedition, which was mounted under Boas' inspiration, direction, and editorship while he was at the American Museum of Natural History, and at Columbia. This project, which was contemporary with the Torres Straits Expedition, resulted in seventeen massive volumes on Siberia and Northwest Coast North America by various people (with an eighteenth still to be published) and far outweighs Torres Straits in its significance for the development of modern ethnological research.

There is another side to Boas as a scientist – the fact that he was a *citizen*-scientist. His careers as citizen and scientist are interwoven. He accepted a moral obligation to spread scientific knowledge as widely as possible, and he himself applied anthropological findings to human problems in education, race relations, nationalism and internationalism, war and peace, and the struggle for democracy and intellectual freedom.

In his first general book, *The Mind of Primitive Man,* the first words of the 1911 first edition are: "Proud of his wonderful achievements, civilized man looks down upon the humbler members of mankind." The last words on the last page read:

I hope the discussions outlined in these pages have shown that the data of anthropology teach us a greater tolerance of forms of civilization different from our own, that we should learn to look on foreign races with greather sympathy and with a conviction that, as all races have contributed in the past to cultural progress in one way or another, so they will be capable of advancing the interests of mankind if we are only willing to give them a fair opportunity (Boas 1911b:278).

Later, in *Anthropology and Modern Life* (1928), he applied anthropological knowledge to racism, nationalism, eugenics, crime and education. Still later, in *Race and Democratic Society,* published posthumously by his son in 1945, some of his hundreds of contributions to widely read magazines and newspapers were brought together.

Boas' commitment to active citizenship and social, liberal ideals began in his childhood home, enriched by the liberalism and free thought of his father and mother. Both had given up all formal religious activity and affiliation, and as Boas later recalled, he and his sisters were "spared the struggle against religious dogma that besets the lives of so many young people." With "an intense interest in nature," Boas was able to approach the world around him with an open mind, without religious preconceptions or inhibitions (Boas 1938a:201).

At twenty-five, while on his expedition to Baffinland, he wrote in a diary of letters that he sent to his fiancée,

Science alone is not the greatest good (June 27, 1883). I believe one can be really happy only as a member of humanity as a whole, if one works with all one's energy together with the masses toward high goals (December 13, 1883). And what I want, for what I want to live and die, is equal rights for all. Equal possibilities to learn and work for rich and poor alike. Don't you believe that to have done even the smallest bit for this is more than all science taken together? (January 22, 1884).

And he added,

I do not think I would be allowed to do this in Germany [and] I do not wish for a German professorship because I would be restricted to my science and to teaching, for which I have no inclination. I should much prefer to live in America and to further these ideas.[3]

It was in 1887 that circumstances combined to make it possible for him to remain in the United States when he returned to New York after a Northwest Coast trip – to marry, to apply for American citizenship (which he obtained five years later), and to begin his American career with the same "American dream" he shared with so many other immigrants to the United States.

Boas' active citizenship did not end with his effort to make his scientific work relevant to human affairs. He was active in matters of principles and in specific situations involving injustice and violations of academic freedom. He resigned from his first teaching position – at Clark University – in a joint protest with other faculty members against continuing infringement of academic freedom by the president, G. Stanley Hall. In his view, a college or university consisted of its faculty and students; trustees and nonacademic administrators were not inherent in it.

A first major test of his principles came in 1914, with the outbreak of World War I. Boas, a pacifist, opposed the war from the beginning. He saw it as fundamentally an imperialist war. In a series of letters to newspapers, he urged that the United States and Woodrow Wilson take the lead in forming a coalition of neutral countries to bring about a ceasefire, and he argued against actions by President Wilson that he charged were leading the United States into the war. In 1917, after the United States declared war, he denounced the action and Wilson in the press.

Boas was not pro-German, as of course was charged. I will support this with a single letter, a letter he wrote to his son Ernst from the field in British Columbia, a few days after the outbreak of war. It is a personal letter, from father to son; it was handwritten and clearly never intended to get the public hearing I am giving it now.

Dear Ernst:
. . . You can imagine that I can think of nothing else than the unfortunate war and the danger to which our aunts and grandmother are exposed. To me it seems like a terrible dream. I cannot visualize how reasonable people and nations which

are "leaders of civilization" can conjure up such a terrible war. If Germany loses, such hatred will be created that it will stir up her nationalism for years to come; if she is victorious, such arrogance, that it will lead to the same consequence. If people would only realize what a source of hatred and misfortune the highly praised patriotism represents! That one cherishes one's own way of life is a natural thing. But does one need to nourish the thought that it is the best of all, that everything that is different is not good but useless, that it is right to despise the people of other nations? In our private lives we would not follow such an unethical rule. Why should it prevail in our national life? If one could only exclude this "patriotismus" from our schools and teach our children the good in our culture, and appreciation of the good in other cultures. Instead they artificially cultivate envy and rivalry (August 16, 1914; APS, 3).

During the war, Boas took public leadership of an effort to counteract wartime hysteria against German culture. Officially, all things German were condemned. The German language ceased to be taught in American schools. Orchestras eliminated German music from their programs. Boas once made a particular request of a conductor to include a certain Beethoven opus in his next concert; the conductor replied that he felt as Boas did about the quality of that opus, but regretted that it was impossible for him to perform it. Boas took the position that as an anthropologist he could not accept the identification of the art and literature of a people with its political administration at a particular time. Heine, Schiller, Bach, and other German artists represented cultural achievements and values that had nothing to do with the Kaiser. It was this position that he took with his students. When Columbia's president Nicholas Murray Butler, ardently prowar and anti-German, instituted spying on what professors did and said, Boas responded by writing a full statement of his views and distributing it in mimeograph to all who came to his classes or requested it.

Boas was not alone at Columbia in his pacifism and antiwar ideas. After the 1917 U.S. declaration of war, when a draft to mobilize an army was being readied, J. McKeen Cattell, a professor of psychology, sent copies of a letter he had written to every member of the U.S. House and Senate. The letter urged that a military draft act provide exemption for those who objected to military service outside the continental borders of the United States. The letter was written on Columbia University stationery. President Butler terminated Cattell on twenty-four hours notice, making forfeit his right to tenure and his accumulations toward retirement. Faculty support for Cattell was immediate. Boas and John Dewey were members of a Cattell Committee, which worked in his support for years. Two other faculty members, James Harvey Robinson and Charles Beard, resigned and joined in the establishment of the New School for Social Research.

In the end, Cattell took his case against Columbia to court and won a complete victory, Columbia settling out of court to avoid publicity. It was so quiet an ending to the case that many did not know and do not know that Columbia had lost its first case on academic rights.

Perhaps the most critical controversy involving Boas and World War I came in 1919, after the war, when he published the following letter in *The Nation*.

Scientists as Spies
To the Editor of *The Nation*

Sir:
In his war address to Congress, President Wilson dwelt at great length on the theory that only autocracies maintain spies, that these are not needed in democracies. At the time that the President made this statement, the government of the United States had in its employ spies of unknown number. I am not concerned here with the familiar discrepancies between the President's words and the actual facts, although we may perhaps have to accept his statement as meaning correctly that we live under an autocracy, that our democracy is a fiction. The point against which I wish to enter a vigorous protest is that a number of men who follow science as their profession, men whom I refuse to designate any longer as scientists, have prostituted science by using it as a cover for their activities as spies.

A soldier whose business is murder as a fine art, a diplomat whose calling is based on deception and secretiveness, a politician whose very life consists in compromises with his conscience, a business man whose aim is personal profit within the limits allowed by a lenient law – such may be excused if they set patriotic devotion above common everyday decency and perform services as spies. They merely accept the code of morality to which modern society still conforms. Not so the scientist. The very essence of his life is the service of truth. We all know scientists who in private life do not come up to the standard of truthfulness, but who nevertheless would not consciously falsify the results of their researches. It is bad enough if we have to put up with these, because they reveal a lack of strength of character that is liable to distort the results of their work. A person, however, who uses science as a cover for political spying, who demeans himself to pose before a foreign government as an investigator and asks for assistance in his alleged researches in order to carry on, under his cloak, his political machinations, prostitutes science in an unpardonable way and forfeits the right to be classed as a scientist.

By accident, incontrovertible proof has come to my hands that at least four men who carry on anthropological work, while employed as government agents, introduced themselves to foreign governments as representatives of scientific researches. They have not only shaken the belief in the truthfulness of science, but they have also done the greatest possible disservice to scientific inquiry. In consequence of their acts, every nation will look with distrust upon the visiting foreign investigator who wants to do honest work, suspecting sinister designs. Such action has raised a new barrier against the development of international friendly co-operation.

Franz Boas
New York, October 16

In the light of controversies over ethics within the American Anthropological Association in recent years, this letter seems a direct and simple plea for scientific integrity. Its anti-Wilson innuendos were not new. Boas had opposed World War I openly and had criticized Wilson's policies in letter after letter in the *New York Times*.

However, Boas' letter in *The Nation* was denounced by the Anthropological Society of Washington in a lengthy statement to the American Anthropological Association at its meeting in December, 1919. The Harvard-Cambridge anthropology group sided with the Washington society. The statement of the Washington group read as follows:

Resolutions of the Anthropological Society of Washington
The attention of the Anthropological Society of Washington having been called to an open letter published in *The Nation* of December 20th by Dr. Franz Boas under the title, "Scientists as Spies," and after said article was read and duly considered, the following resolution was adopted and ordered to be submitted to the American Anthropological Association at its meeting in Boston; to Section H of the American Association for the Advancement of Science meeting in St. Louis; and to the Archeological Institute of America meeting in Pittsburgh, with the request that suitable action be taken by these associations. Also that a copy of this resolution be sent to *The Nation* and *Science* with a request for its publication.

Resolved: That the article in question unjustly criticizes the President of the United States and attacks the fundamental principles of American democracy; that the reflections contained in the article fall on all American anthropologists who have been anywhere outside the limits of the United States during the last five years; that the information thus given is liable to have future serious effects on the work of all anthropologists outside the boundaries of the United States; and that the accusation, given such prominent publicity and issuing from such a source, will doubtless receive wide attention and is liable to prejudice foreign governments against all scientific men coming from this country to their respective territories, particularly if under government auspices; therefore *Be it resolved,* that in the opinion of the Council of the Anthropological Society of Washington, the publication of the article in question was unwarranted and will prove decidedly injurious to the interests of American scientists in general; that the author has shown himself inconsiderate to the best interests of his American colleagues who may be obliged to carry on research in foreign countries, and that his action therefore deserves our emphatic disapproval.

At the meeting, after a great deal of discussion, the following resolution was moved instead of the long statement from the Washington Anthropological Society:

*Resolved:*That the expression of opinion by Dr. Franz Boas contained in an open letter to the editor of *The Nation* on the date of October 16, 1919, and published in the issue of that weekly for December 20, 1919, is unjustified and does not represent the opinion of the American Anthropological Association. *Be it further resolved:* That a copy of this resolution be forwarded to the Executive Board of the National Research Council and such other scientific associations as may have taken action on this matter.

I have presented the text of Boas' letter and if anyone can find a word in it that says it represents anybody's views but his own, I would like to know it. It was a personal statement of his convictions, and it involved no one else. He did not name the persons he was referring to. Nevertheless, Boas was censured, by a vote of about two to one.

The Washington Anthropological Society distributed its original statement widely, in spite of the fact that it had not been passed by the AAA. A great deal of the rancor aroused was allegedly due to Boas' publication of a professional statement in a public, nonprofessional magazine. Yet Boas had sent it earlier to *Science*, which was then edited by J. McKeen Cattell, the same Cattell who had been kicked out of Columbia for his pacifist letter to Congress on Columbia stationery. Cattell replied:

I fear I must decide that it would not be advisable to print the letter entitled "Scientists as Spies" in *Science*. I of course concur in all that you say, but it seems to me desirable for *Science* to avoid, especially at the present time, all questions of a political character, even though they do relate to scientific matters.

> Sincerely,
> J. McKeen Cattell

I don't know how Boas felt about that letter, but he sent his statement right off to Henry Raymond Mussey, a friend who was editor of *The Nation*. Mussel immediately accepted it for publication and wrote to Boas:

Thank you very much for your disturbing letter on "Scientists as Spies" sent us for publication. It is indeed a distressing thing that scientific men should stoop to such dishonorable practices, and I am very glad indeed to have the opportunity of giving publicity to your protest.

That is how Boas' letter happened to appear in *The Nation* rather than in *Science*.

There is a final note to this early controversy over professional ethics. The next month (on January 9, 1920), Cattell published in *Science* the full text of the communication from the Washington Anthropological Society, in the form that had been *rejected* by the AAA meeting.

I close this page of history by noting that one scientist wrote the Washington Anthropological Society to ask, in view of the statement it had circulated and had asked everybody to act upon, whether Boas' charges in the *Nation* letter were true. He noted that the Washington group had made no reference to that question at all.

Following his censure, Boas resigned as representative of the American Anthropological Association to the National Research Council, who accepted the resignation regretfully. Apart from this, I have no evidence that his participation in the AAA was ever terminated, even transiently. Annual reports of the Association in succeeding years show him still to be a member of various committees that he had been on previously.

Stocking has treated this incident in the context of "The Scientific Reaction Against Cultural Anthropology, 1917–1920," the title of a paper in his book *Race, Culture, and Evolution* (1968). He focuses on the manner in which opposition to the development of Boas' cultural anthropology, fortified by the jealousy of his achievements, caused the *Nation* letter to be used as an excuse for violent anti-Boas action. I think the letter also stands as an example of Boas in action on issues of scientific ethics.

Over the years, as Boas became known through his work and public statements as a strong liberal on academic and political issues and on race relations, he accepted board memberships on and allowed the use of his name by many public-service citizens' organizations and ad hoc committees. He also organized some of his own. His main means of action was to make public statements to the press or through letters to the press, or to form a committee which then took public or private action as the matter required. It was in this way that Boas initiated two large-scale national actions in relation to the rise of Hitler and Nazism. The first followed a Nazi denunciation of Jewish science. Boas responded with a public statement signed by over 8,000 American scientists, affirming that there was only one science, to which religion and race were irrelevant. Later, after Hitler came to power in 1933 and Boas' books (among others) were burned, Boas organized a group at Columbia called the Committee for Democracy and Intellectual Freedom. The idea spread rapidly to other universities, where chapters were formed, until the committee had more than 11,000 members.

Boas also joined other American scientists in organizing committees to help scientific refugees from Hitler's Germany and other countries overrun by the Nazis. The primary effort was to find the refugee scientists positions in the United States or elsewhere in the free world. Boas was engaged in this activity at the moment he died in December 1942. Along with Lévi-Strauss, Boas had arranged a luncheon at Columbia in honor of Paul Rivet, refugee linguist from Vichy France. Boas suddenly collapsed, in Lévi-Strauss' arms, and died even as he was in the middle of a sentence about a new idea on race.

A major part of Boas' scientific work and its application concerned race and race relations, especially the problems of the American Negro. He was probably the first scientist to publish that Negro and White were fundamentally equal, as were all so-called races. He embodied this view in the title of one paper, "The Genetic Basis for Democracy" (Boas 1940b). American Negro leaders, organizations, and universities were quick to recognize in Boas a source of strength. For W. E. B. DuBois, a founder of the NAACP and editor of its publication *Crisis,* Boas wrote a paper for the first issue of that magazine, on the Negro and the race problem in America (Boas 1910). He gave a commencement address at Atlanta University in 1906. He participated in the organization and work of the Association for the Study of Negro Life and History and its publication *The Journal of Negro History,* and later of the Council on African Affairs, of which Paul Robeson was chairman and Max Yergan director.

As an indication of what such Afro-American leaders thought of Boas, I have a message Max Yergan sent to Helene Boas after Boas died:

Mrs. Helene Yampolsky
Grantwood, N.J.
On behalf of the Council on African Affairs, I express deepest regrets over the death of your father. He was a guide and inspiration to us in our deliberation and activities for the welfare of African peoples. The work of organizations like ours is possible because Franz Boas has lived (APS, 4).

I began this discussion by selecting four principal points for emphasis. I have touched on three: (1) that Boas was the architect of modern anthropology; (2) that the element in his training and experience that made him the modernizer of the study of man was the empirical way of thinking of natural history; and (3) that Boas was a *citizen-scientist* who applied the work of anthropology to problems of society, and was an activist on academic and political issues – in both ways serving as a model for anthropology as a humanitarian science.

I come now to my final theme, Boas as theorist. Far from being antitheory, Boas was himself, I would argue, the great theorist of modern anthropology, who established the core of anthropological theory on which the science is based.

Inescapably, discussions of Boas on theory must begin with his handling of the theory of evolution. Here are his words on that subject in 1888:

The development of ethnology is largely due to the general recognition of the principle of biological evolution. It is a common feature of all forms of evolutionary theory that every living being is considered as the result of an historical development. The fate of an individual does not influence himself alone, but also all succeeding generations. . . . This point of view introduced an historical perspective into the natural sciences and revolutionized their methods. The development of ethnology is largely due to the adoption of the evolutionary standpoint, because it impressed the conviction upon us that no event in the life of a people passes without leaving its effect upon later generations. The myths told by our ancestors and in which they believed have left their impress upon the ways of thinking of their descendants (Boas 1940a:633).

Clearly, in his early anthropological thinking Boas (1) accepted biological evolution as scientifically valid, (2) understood evolution in *historical* terms, not as orthogenetic, and (3) affirmed evolution as a *first principle* of ethnology and anthropology.

These statements must be emphasized in view of oft-repeated assertions that Boas was antievolutionary. No statement could show more clearly that he not only accepted evolution but accepted it as basic. Yet he did reject the so-called evolutionary ideas of some anthropologists. What did he reject, as distinct from the evolution that he affirmed?

In *Primitive Art* he wrote,

Evolution, meaning the continuous change of thought and action, or historic continuity, cannot be accepted unreservedly. It is otherwise when it is conceived as meaning the universally valid continuous development of one cultural form out of a preceding type (Boas 1927:80).

Essentially he was opposing orthogenesis, which is defined as follows by Webster's dictionary:

In biology, variations which in successive generations of an organism, follow some particular line, evolving some new type irrespective of natural selection or other external factor. Determinate variation or evolution. Sociologically, the theory that social evolution always follows the same direction and passes through the same stages in each culture despite differing external conditions.

Orthogenesis, by its very definition, is a contradiction of Darwin's theory of evolution. Darwin based evolutionary change on the principle of natural selection; among the vast number of variations occurring in each new generation, some were "selected" to survive and reproduce, others were not. Natural selection in turn must be understood as historical in character. Forms or species are subject to variation and change. So, too, is the environment in which they occur. The interaction between variations of form and the changing environment is an event of a particular time, not predetermined by either system. In modern biology, orthogenesis is not a fundamental evolutionary process. The point is made in Simpson's *Meaning of Evolution* (1950:22) and in various other treatments.

It was this distinction between orthogenesis and evolution in its historical, Darwinian sense that Boas had in mind, as has been noted by some. Washburn has written about this, referring to "evolution" as the term was used by Tylor, Spencer, Morgan, and their contemporary throwbacks. "There is no evolution in the traditional anthropological sense. What Boas referred to as evolution was orthogenesis, which receives no support from modern genetic theory. What the geneticist sees as evolution is far closer to what Boas called history than to what he called evolution" (Washburn 1963:522). In an article on Boas I wrote, "Boas' critique was directed not against the principle of evolution as historical development, which he accepted, but against the orthogenesis of dominant English and American theory of the time. He opposed history to orthogenesis" (Lesser 1968a:101).

Boas himself made the distinction in clear terms in several places. In 1920, he wrote in "The Methods of Ethnology":

The hypothesis [of evolution in traditional anthropology] implies the thought that our modern Western European civilization represents the highest cultural development toward which all other more primitive cultural types tend, and that therefore retrospectively we construct an *orthogenetic* development towards our modern civilization (Boas 1940a:282; italics mine).

In 1919, in a discussion at an American Ethnological Society meeting, Boas is reported by the Secretary, Robert H. Lowie, to have spoken as follows:

Professor Boas pointed out that in comparing the doctrines of unilinear evolutionists to those of biologists we are not quite fair to the biologists, since they do not postulate a single line of evolution without any divergences; what the cultural theorists of the earlier period did was to stress the *orthogenetic* character of cultural evolution.[4]

In 1938, discussing problems of the laws of historic development, Boas wrote:

When these data are assembled, the question arises whether they present an orderly picture or whether history proceeds haphazardly; in other words, whether an *orthogenetic* development of human forms may be discovered, and whether a regular sequence of stages of historical development may be recognized (Boas 1938b:3; italics mine).

Several aspects of this view of evolution help explain Boas' view of theory and his work as a scientific theorist. First, he uses the fact of evolution as proof "that every living being is the result of an historical development." He understands evolution as history and as evidence of the historicity of living things. In effect, Boas' view is a major theory, both of culture and of man. It states that every culture is the result of a long history, and that every such history involves a great complexity of events, accidents of history, and interrelation of factors.

In relation to Boas' view of evolution as basic to anthropology, note that he is speaking empirically. The empiricism he brought from natural history studies called for generalizations or scientific theories that are *inductive* – that come out of the data and that serve to bind them together.

As Darwin's theory of evolution expressed in a generalization both the continuity and change of living forms – *descent with modification* – so a similar theory of the historical evolution of cultures served to express their continuity through time and their diversification and change – the idea of *continuity with change*.

Additionally, Boas established the modern *theory* of culture. Stocking (1968, 1974) has shown that it was Boas who established the modern use and meaning of the term. But more than that, in doing so he established the central theory of modern anthropology.

When Boas showed that cultures and their diversities could not be explained by differences in outer environment, natural environment, or geography; when he showed that cultural diversity could not be explained by differences in inner makeup of human groups (the racial argument); and finally, when he showed that cultural diversity was not a matter of stages of predetermined development or orthogenetic evolution, he made cultures and their histories the primary determinants of diversities or similarities at any time. Cultures became the basic factor in the understanding of cultural man. In anthropological thinking and explanation, the concept *cultural* replaced the concept *natural*. The culture concept did away at one blow with efforts to explain human nature biologically and physiologically (as with concepts of instinct or of inherent drives).

I would suggest, then, that two great theories in anthropology were contributed by Boas: the idea that in culture history, culture is the primary determinant, rather than some noncultural independent variable; and the theory of culture in its modern sense, as learned behavior. Both of these are inductive theories, based on the comparison and contrast of human cultures.

The immense influence of this anthropological discovery and development is indicated, for example, by John Dewey in his article, "Human Nature":

Anthropology, on the other hand, has made it clear that the varieties of cultural and institutional forms which have existed are not to be traced to anything which can be called unmodified human nature, but are the products of interaction with the social environment. They are functions, in the mathematical sense, of institutional organization and cultural traditions, as these operate to shape raw biological material into definitively human shape.

If we accept the extreme partisan stand, it may be regarded as now generally accepted that the immense diversities of culture which have existed and which still exist cannot possibly be derived directly from any stock of original powers and impulses, that the problem is one of explaining in its own terms the diversification of the cultural milieus which act upon original nature.

As this fact gains recognition, the problem of modifiability is being placed upon the same level as the persistence of custom or tradition. It is wholly a matter of empirical determination, not of *a priori* theorizing (Dewey 1932:536).

Dewey adds further on:

The present controversies between those who assert the essential fixity of human nature and those who believe in a great measure of modifiability center chiefly around the future of war and the future of a competitive economic system motivated by private profit. It is justifiable to say without dogmatism that both anthropology and history give support to those who wish to change these institutions. It is demonstrable that many of the obstacles to change which have been attributed to human nature are in fact due to the inertia of institutions and to the voluntary desire of powerful classes to maintain the existing status (Dewey 1932:536).

In Boas' own view of theory (in the sense of scientific generalizations or laws), as he outlined it in his early paper "The Study of Geography" (1887), he made the historical character of human phenomena basic (Boas 1940a:639–47). The goal in such a field of study is "the thorough understanding of phenomena"; in other places he speaks of "complex phenomena." Regularities or generalizations which are discoverable are viewed pragmatically, not as an end in themselves, but as an additional tool in analysis. This, I suggest, is not an antitheory or antigeneralization position, but a reversal of emphasis. He suggests that in the complex field of human cultural history, theory – read laws or generalizations – is not the end, but, where discoverable, one means among others to be used in scientific analysis and for the understanding of phenomena.

As a generalizer in his own right, Boas is the most generalizing anthropologist I have read. I once wrote a paper called "Research Procedure and the Laws of Culture" [see Chapter 2], in which I tried to show the nature of laws as working assumptions. I limited myself to selected illustrations from Boas, because he was supposed to be nontheoretical. I found most of the illustrations in the lengthy article he wrote years ago for the *Encyclopedia of the Social Sciences* on "Anthropology" (Boas 1930a). In that article, on every phase of the subject, he tries to generalize as much as possible what the import of the data is. The article is full of generalizations, some of which even take the specific form of attempts to state laws. I think it is important to realize that a generalization for him was arrived at inductively and was an attempt to sum up, to pull together, the meanings of the many facts so far known. In practice, it was always subject to further questions, further inquiries, further verification.

Boas moved onward from problem to problem throughout his active scientific life. He taught his students to attempt to do the same. He left anthropology an open field of inquiry, its methods rooted in empirical observation and experience, its goal an even wider and deeper knowledge of many, its ideal – contributions toward a better world for all men.

2   Research procedure and the laws of culture

I

When discussions of scientific method shift from natural sciences to social sciences, we tend to feel that we are turning from strict sciences to subject matters which may have achieved some measure of intellectual competence but which lack the rigor, objectivity and principles of organization found in mature science. This sense of a difference between the natural sciences and the social sciences is connected with questions of the meaning and role of laws. To the extent to which social and historical events have not been reduced to laws or perhaps cannot be, the disciplines which study such events are considered immature or imperfect sciences. To the extent to which social sciences do not offer predictions, they are felt to have little application to the solution of actual and immediate problems. When a bridge has to be built over a chasm, the laws of the natural sciences can be brought to bear. But when a treaty is to be drawn, where, it is asked, are the social and historical laws which can be applied to the situation?

Laws as statements of some observed regularity in conditions are based upon experience. The experience of order and consistency of some form is prior to the affirmation of the existence of law, and laws when made explicit are formulations of regularities which have been experienced. In all types of experience we base present action upon past experience, constantly anticipating and frequently finding our expectations fulfilled. This is as true in the analysis of social and historical events, and in ordinary social experience, as it is in the physical and chemical dimension. Hence we cannot deny that on the plane of the social and historical we

This paper was read at the Second Conference on Methods in Philosophy and the Sciences, New School for Social Research, New York, November 1937; and at the Annual Meetings of the Central Section of the American Anthropological Association, Milwaukee, Wis., April 1938. It was originally published in *Philosophy of Science* 6:345–55. © 1939 The Williams and Wilkins Co. Reproduced by permission.

experience order and consistency without affirming as a principle that social and historical events are completely disordered, inconsistent and chaotic. *Some* order and consistency *is* experienced. Therefore, to deny the existence of social and historical laws cannot mean that no regularities are found in such phenomena. Nor, furthermore, can such denial mean that regularities exist but cannot be discovered, since we accept ordered events as existent only because we have experienced such phenomena. Obviously we should be able to find some mode of statement for regularities which we experience. The denial of laws in social and historical events, then, can mean only that we have not as yet succeeded in adequately defining orders and regularities, and that this seems a difficult task.

It cannot be denied that social sciences have thus far failed to formulate statements of order and regularity comparable to the laws of the natural sciences. Where claims for laws have been made they have not received the universality of acceptance from other workers in the same field, which is one of the criteria of validity. But so far as social sciences have failed, their failure cannot be credited to the absence of phenomenal regularities on the social plane and must therefore involve shortcomings in methodology and technique.

Traditional concepts of the nature of laws may be involved in the difficulties of the social scientist. Many think of laws as statements of underlying processes which determine cases observed. Something of the older idea that there may be moving purposes in events is involved. When attempts are made to define laws, the procedure usually moves on the plane of discovering general and all-embracing principles of conditions or developments. Attention tends to be turned away from actual phenomena studied and the obvious and thoroughly accepted beliefs which may be held about it, and toward some special realm of hidden linkages in which laws may be expected to lie. When hidden connections prove hard to discover, there is a tendency to profess a disbelief in laws. Nevertheless the actual procedures of investigators belie such professed statements. The scientist must in practice approach the materials of any given case or problem with certain expectations based upon his past experience and analyses. These expectations or anticipations are not only involved in the terms and concepts used, but include also ways of attacking the problem and a whole body of already accepted ideas about the nature of such phenomenal conditions.

This general fact about empirical procedure is no less true in the social sciences than in the natural or physical sciences. It is as apparent in the work of the social anthropologist studying culture and society as in any other field of social investigation. Unaware of or oblivious to the body of accepted beliefs with which he works as the anthropologist may be, general truths about culture and society can be illustrated from every phase of the anthropological field by drawing upon the fund of "normal expectations" of the anthropologist at work. In offering a sample selection of such expectations, I am intentionally using the obvious, so that illustrations presented can hardly be called in question if their terms are understood.

II

Under aboriginal conditions of life the only modes of communication are those by personal contact. We observe that wherever peoples are in contact, they borrow from or imitate one another's customs and institutions. Hence a major anticipation in research is that unless recent movements of peoples have occurred in an area, the culture of any group will resemble that of its neighbors. A greater degree of resemblance is expected the longer the time period of continuous and undisturbed contact. At the same time, in historical analysis we find that the origins of every culture or civilization have been diverse. In research practice these expectations mean that we prepare for the study of a particular group, who are as yet unknown, by finding out all we can about its neighbors and the general area in which it is located. When we study the particular tribe, we look for special historical conditions to explain marked deviations from the norms of culture for the area.

In any cultural group, because of the way in which the individual is conditioned by the behavior of others among whom he grows up, we expect the behavior of the individual to conform to the behavior patterns of his group, or, in somewhat different phrasing, we expect the behavior of the individual to fall within the range of behavior patterns of the group. Furthermore, in terms of behavior patterns, an individual selected at random is expected to prove a more complete microcosm of his group, the more homogeneous the culture. In field practice this means that we rely on evidence based on a limited number of informants or cases the more, the more homogeneous the culture.

Among institutional forms, the universality of a sex division of labor and of an incest rule are suggestive. In any society adult economic occupations or activities are differentiated in some way according to sex. Again, in any society a differentiation occurs between members of the opposite sex with whom sexual relations and/or marriage are socially acceptable and those with whom they are not.

In many phases of culture, as for example in art, we expect certain types of consistency. The recognition of style in the art products of a given people means that if we have examined a limited number of specimens we expect unexamined specimens to conform in many predictable ways to consistencies of style and content discovered in the samples studied. If in a dozen baskets or pots we find the use of several geometrical motives, we expect further specimens to show other geometrical motives and perhaps repetition of some already noted. If another specimen were to differ both in style of arrangement of elements, and content as regards motives used, we would question whether it actually had been made by artists of the same cultural group. Illustrations of similar types of consistency could I think equally well be drawn from literary forms, ritual patterns, music, kinship modes of behavior and other phases.

Under aboriginal conditions, in many cases little or no trade in essentials is carried on, and there are many situations in which transportation is at a minimum. The environment in such cases affects culture directly. We may say that: The resources of the local environment of any cultural group constitute limitations of the technology and material culture in inverse ratio to the degre to which trade and transportation are developed. In many primitive cultures, in the absence of techniques of food storage and preservation, the food quest is necessarily continuous, and no prolonged periods of leisure can be expected. We study social and political institutions under such conditions in terms of the limitations set by a continuous food quest and the absence of leisure. There are also expectations regarding political institutions under certain conditions. Thus, for example, Boas suggests:

In a region of ample food supply in which the maintenance of life depends solely upon physical skill and in which a sparse population allows everyone to find a productive hunting ground, a differentiation according to rank or wealth is not likely to occur, except insofar as orphans, widows and old people may be thrown upon the mercy of their friends and relatives (Boas 1930a:100).

The world-wide system of production and exchange which we know today is a recent phenomenon. Among aboriginal peoples, in only a few regions are cultural groups dependent parts of a large, intertribal system of exchange. The more general tendency is toward relatively independent, self-sufficient groups. Where that is the condition, the density of population is linked to the form and character of the economy, a fact emphasized by many writers. Boas discusses this in the following:

We may recognize definite, causally determined relations between the economic conditions of a people and the size of the population. The number of individuals of a hunting tribe inhabiting a particular territory is obviously limited by the available amount of game. There will be starvation as soon as the population exceeds the maximum that may be maintained in an unfavorable year. If the same people develop agriculture and the art of preserving a food supply for a long period, a denser population is possible, and, at the same time, each individual will have more leisure and there will be a greater number of individuals enjoying lesiure. Under these conditions the population is liable to increase. We may perhaps say that complexity of culture and absolute number of individuals constituting a population are correlated. Whether this development actually occurs in a given population is an entirely different question (Boas 1928:210).

In other words, complexity of culture cannot be expected unless some degree of population density is found, but populations may conceivably be large and culture relatively simple.

Expectations as regards the forms of property and ownership can be illustrated. Whenever complete objects are manufactured by individuals, if the individual maker is not a slave, has not been hired, and has not been delegated, the objects he makes are his for use and disposition, and such individual ownership is socially sanctioned. As regards my own experience of the data, I would affirm that in a region of uniform economic conditions involving hunting and food-gathering peoples who lack arts of storage and preservation, raiding for property does not occur. Boas notes that "whenever the transfer of property involves future obligations on the part of the recipient, the transaction is public and gives opportunity to the development of ritualistic behavior" (Boas 1930a:100).

Many illustrations of expected relations could probably be drawn from the more technical field of primitive social organization. In fact it is in respect to this aspect of culture, particularly as regards forms of marriage and social organization, that there is a long history of attempts from Morgan's day to the present to define consistent iterrelations or laws. Rivers, for example, asserted in a classic passage in relation to the "determination of the nomenclature of relationship by social conditions," that "we have here a case in which the principle of determinism applies with a rigour and definiteness equal to that of any of the exact sciences" (Rivers 1914:93). As an illustrative suggestion in this field I would state that where prescribed primary marriages are the social rule, affinal kinship terms and usages will reveal the character of the prescribed marriage. Native Australia is of course a main case in point, where rules prescribe the marriage of certain kinds of cousins. As a result, relatives by marriage are also relatives by consanguinity, and terms and usages for relationships reveal the facts. In practice the principle I have mentioned means that if a field worker were to report the existence of a rule of marriage among a certain tribe, yet could not describe the form of the rule, we could infer the nature of the rule from the kinship terms and usages for relatives by marriage. If no consistent marriage pattern were implied by them, we would doubt the existence of any prescribed rule of primary marriage.

Boas indicates a specific expectation as regards marriage forms: "If polygyny is combined with permanent matrilocal residence, the wives must necessarily be sisters" (Boas 1930a:87).

The field of religion could be drawn upon also for illustration. For example, a theological systematization of religious thoughts and concepts cannot be expected in the absence of a priesthood. Or, quoting Boas on the reinterpretation of traditional behavior and belief, "It may be claimed as a general rule that interpretations of customs and attitudes do not agree with their historical origin but are based on the general cultural tendencies of the time when the interpretation is given" (Boas 1928:213ff.).[5] The general experience of investigators of the functional role of ceremonial and ritual forms has been commented on by various writers. Boas summarizes the basic situation by saying:

Important actions, when accompanied by difficulty of execution and likelihood of failure, or those involving danger, give rise to a variety of types of ceremonial behavior. The making of a canoe is often an act of great ceremonial importance, as in Polynesia, or is accompanied by superstitious beliefs and practices, as on the Northwest Coast of America. Hunting and fishing on which the sustenance of the people depends, agricultural pursuits, herding and war expeditions, are almost always connected with more or less elaborate ceremonials and complex beliefs, on the whole the more so the more deeply success or failure affect the life of the people. We may recognize an expression of the same "law" in the formal celebrations with which we like to accompany the achievement of great technical undertakings, the completion of the education of the young, or the opening of an important assembly (Boas 1928:214).[5a]

Perhaps most controversy has surrounded questions of laws of development and of predictions about the future. Here too, however, one can illustrate how experienced consistencies have affected our expectations. While we do not accept the exact sequences postulated in early schemes of the evolution of economic forms, we can nevertheless assert that in historical development the presence of certain forms necessarily implies the earlier presence of certain others. For example, any culture with agricultural or pastoral techniques must have been in a condition without them at some time of its historical past, viz., in some condition of hunting, fishing, food-gathering economy in which resources of nature were garnered as found. Cultures which are complex, with specialized institutions and an intensive division of labor, necessarily imply a historical past of simpler institutional forms and less specialization.

The possibility of prediction about the future is often denied. Yet consider cases such as the following: We know from repeated instances that wherever in island regions of Melanesia certain forms of imperialistic exploitation have been practiced on native groups, certain types of economic and cultural breakdown have occurred. The same methods of exploitation are now being carried out in New Guinea that were used many years ago in other Melanesian areas. In interior New Guinea there are still peoples who have never been seen by Europeans. We can predict that, when these groups are discovered, if they are exploited in the same imperialistic modes which were used elsewhere in the region, certain definite conditions of cultural breakdown will rapidly follow.

III

These somewhat random examples illustrate the character of normal expectations that are basic in contemporary anthropological research. If anthropologists were in the habit of making expectations more explicit, I believe that illustrations could be multiplied indefinitely.

The role of such expectations in inquiry and research is in the first place similar to the role of expectations in ordinary experience. Anticipations based on past experience are used, consciously or unconsciously, in dealing with present or impending situations. But further, such expectations are of the nature of hypotheses, linking former investigations and research to the case in hand. Whether explicitly stated, or implicitly felt, they affect inquiry and treatment, determining to a large extent what we take for granted and where we give special attention to unusual phenomena. These expectations of the investigator reflect the consistencies and types of order or invariant relations that have been so far experienced by him. If framed as hypotheses, in such form that they can be subjected to verification in any given case, they become essentially the laws with which the investigator is actually operating in his research.

In the study of peoples and cultures, these normal expectations of the investigator are usually the last things to be made overt. They are most of the time somewhat unconscious. Attention is directed not at them but at something else, viz., the particular and special conditions of the particular and specific case. Thus arises the tendency in modern anthropology toward a cultural atomism which seeks to describe the particularity and uniqueness of the special culture without realizing that its very difference from other conditions can be rendered adequately only against the background of its similarities to them. In spite of its uniqueness it is a society and a culture and there are many features implied by that fact alone, which are too often disregarded as over-obvious. Hence, instead of the particular case serving as an experiment in terms of which expectations can be consciously verified or disproved, it is too apt to be taken as a case which disproves the existence of general homogeneities.

If we turn for laws to the expectations of the scientist at work, the instrumental character of such laws is immediately apparent. Expectations cannot be fixed or final statements of immutable and eternal qualities or relations, but in the form of laws are clearly tools forged by the investigator in his experience and work by means of which he seeks to bring to bear the fruit of his earlier experience in the analysis and control of the present case. In so doing the present case takes on new meaning. In relation to laws as hypotheses or working expectations, the case which is studied at any time becomes the experiment by means of which the hypotheses are verified or disproved. Hence every specific and controlled research performance, if its relation to former cases is exactly charted in terms of hypotheses, constitutes a verification of the whole system or set of hypotheses and laws already realized. At the same time, it offers, because of its particularity, novel conditions which may generate additional expectations or hypotheses. The constant emphasis in social sciences upon research is then seen in its true light. It serves the function of experiment in other sciences, viz., that hypotheses or laws are being checked and verified by the conditions in a specific case.

The fruitfulness of this concept of the nature of laws for anthropology seems to me great. Modern ethnologists tend to emphasize the need for more intensive analyses and studies of specific cultures or areas. But in carrying out such research the usual procedure is to look to each culture to suggest novel and special problems, often tangential to earlier and other work. If expectations are made overt as hypotheses, this turning to intensive analysis of a particular culture has the genuine significance of an experiment in culture, and the special or particular conditions encountered will not be lost sight of, but take on new meaning.

One of the main objections to attempts to frame laws of social and historical phenomena has been that they can have little applicability to actual particular situations. It is claimed that in isolating what is common to many instances, we must necessarily arrive at abstract generalizations which can have little relevance to action in a particular situation, with all its local uniqueness. But if, instead of using methods of progressive abstraction, we approach the problem of laws in terms of normal expectations employed in dealing with a particular case, and subject to verification and disproof in terms of that case, the applicability of the revised expectations to the next particular case is enhanced. Laws as instrumental hypotheses linking past to present experience will have the more applicability to particular situations the more they are used explicitly in action and revised to meet the needs of actions and situations.

Constant practice of such a procedure seems bound to sharpen our awareness of the aspects of our own social experiences which can be framed as hypotheses and subjected to verification or disproof. The keener our awareness becomes the more the social scene is likely to reveal of homogeneity, order and consistency in experience, which can be used in the control of social events and situations. Laws for social action must be derived from actual experience and practice in dealing with social events and phenomena and only then can be expected to have fruitful application to the problems of social life. To derive such laws a fundamental requirement is that we make more explicit the assumptions or expectations which link past experiences to present situations, within any special or technical discipline, and ultimately within the milieu of social experience itself.

Part II

Theory and method

Introduction to Part II

What follow are two of Alexander Lesser's best-known essays. Both were written during his most productive years; both deal with theory and method, rather than field data, in anthropology. But their histories as essays are quite different. "Functionalism in social anthropology" (Chapter 3), published in 1935, is an unusual scholarly product. It attempted to settle a quite specious debate between so-called functionalists and so-called historicists, by suggesting that good anthropological research would take into account both the relationships among different aspects of culture at any one point *in* time and the history of the culture and its institutions *over* time.

Looked at from the perspective of the present, it is difficult to see why such a view should ever have been rejected. But Lesser's paper was given during an epoch when too many anthropologists stood to gain by eschewing either functional analysis on the one hand or historical research on the other. British "functionalist" anthropology was attributed to Bronislaw Malinowski and A. R. Radcliffe-Brown – though neither welcomed the association. It was antihistorical in character, emphasizing the interrelationship among institutions and judging historical "explanation" to be merely an inferior substitute for good fieldwork. American anthropology was based, in large part, on historical inquiry. American anthropologists were not, however, antifunctionalists, neither their historical orientation nor their professional stance required them to be. But the gaps between British and American anthropology were too wide, and the lack of mutual interest too great, to permit any genuine reconciliation.

It was into this difference of viewpoint that Lesser, still quite a junior scholar, tumbled. When in 1977 he looked back on his motives for having written "Functionalism in social anthropology," he was able to see things from a clearer perspective. He had been asked by a colleague at Columbia University, Joan Vincent, to describe to a graduate class on complex societies how he came to write the essay on functionalism. He included an entertaining tale that deserves to be retold at length (though somewhat modified) for the light it throws upon Lesser the person, as well as upon his times and colleagues:

I first met both Radcliffe-Brown and Malinowski in 1926 or 1927. It was the first occasion of their both being in New York at the same time. Pliny Earle Goddard, then Curator of the American Museum of Natural History, and a sort of working associate of Franz Boas, was very anxious to have Radcliffe-Brown and Malinowski meet Boas, with a major thought in mind. He believed they would both discover that Boas was driving at the same thing they were driving at, that there really weren't any fundamental conflicts. He thought that if he could get them together, they would talk, and something would come of it.

At that time, Ruth Bunzel was in the group of graduate students at Columbia. (I had just begun graduate work.) Goddard managed an arrangement by which Radcliffe-Brown and Malinowski were invited to what was a large living room in Ruth Bunzel's parents' apartment, somewhere near Riverside Drive. So they were to meet there, and with them a few graduate students, those who had enough – you know – to get in. There were only about ten of us: six graduate students, Malinowski, Radcliffe-Brown, Goddard and Boas.

We met there, and when the time seemed right, Goddard tried to get some discussion going. He couldn't get Boas to say anything. Boas was very gracious and pleasant to everybody, but he wouldn't say anything. So Goddard invited Malinowski and Radcliffe-Brown to say something. Radcliffe-Brown started off by giving extemporaneously a fifteen-minute exposition of what he considered to be the meaning of meaning. It was, from a verbal standpoint a beautiful performance. Then Goddard sort of turned to Boas: "Well?" Goddard didn't say anything; he just waited. Boas simply looked at Goddard, and looked at Radcliffe-Brown, and nodded his head, and that was all. Then Goddard turned to Malinowski and asked him if he wanted to say anything, and Malinowski gave an exposition of his concept of functionalism. He used some of the same words which appear in his article on anthropology in the *Encyclopaedia Britannica,* and this could have been part of what he said that evening:

> Functional analysis of culture aims at the explanation of anthropological facts at all levels of development by their function, by the part which they play within the integral system of culture, by the manner in which they are related to each other within the system, and by the manner in which this system is related to the physical surroundings. The functional view of culture insists therefore upon the principle that in every type of civilization, every custom, material object, idea, and belief fulfills some vital function, has some task to accomplish, represents an indispensable part within a working whole.

Malinowski said it that night the same way he wrote it here.[6]

After he got through with his fifteen minutes, Goddard turned to Boas, expecting him to say something; and he looked at Malinowski; and he looked at the rest of us – and then there was utter silence. So nothing much was said, and the effort by Goddard to get some kind of discussion going, either between the visitors, or between both of them and Boas, was a complete loss at that point.

Goddard was very anxious to have Malinowski and Radcliffe-Brown and Boas understand each other. He thought, much as we graduate students at Columbia thought, however erroneously, that what we were doing in American ethnology was functional. What we were interested in was perhaps best expressed in print at that time, let's say, by the opening chapters of Benedict's *Patterns of Culture*. We were interested in the relations between one aspect of culture and another. We did not feel that what Malinowski and Radcliffe-Brown had to say was particularly alien; it was a variation, but it wasn't different. We were not interested in the shreds and patches theory Lowie proposes on the last page of his *Primitive Society*.[7] We weren't interested in the computations that Kroeber and others at the University of California were making, counting items of culture and calculating the statistical degree of similarity between two cultures in terms of how the count came out, and so on.[8] Most of us began with an emphasis upon *fieldwork*, which meant observation and an attempt to report *what actually happened* in some group or culture. We considered the famous manual of "anthropological" questions put out in England for government employees (*Notes and Queries*) – to be sure to obtain answers to all these questions – to be nonsense. Each question was an item, and we didn't think that way. We didn't think about culture that way; and this was true not only for kinship studies but for all else – mythology, religion, folklore, and so on. Radcliffe-Brown and Malinowski were not adding anything, in our minds. We hoped the meeting was going to show that Malinowski and Radcliffe-Brown had something to learn about the history of anthropology, and about Boas, and about what we were doing in the United States – that we were trying to understand everything in culture in terms of its context of interrelations. Let me give you an illustration. In their book, *Family and Community in Ireland,* Arensberg and Kimball write:

> Though the work deals with rural communities, the authors do not intend it to be in any sense a community study or social survey. Intensive observation brought the authors into intimate contact with three small communities, whose names will appear very often. But their field work was not directed toward discovering what was particular to these. It was aimed at a larger problem. It was based on an assumption fundamental to anthropological theory today. It assumed that the chief determinant factor in human society may well be human activity itself. The question behind the authors' inquiries was couched in terms of this hypothesis. What could they learn to help them to an explanation of the uniformities of human action by following the influence of one kind of activity of human culture upon another? Their results have thus always the same general form: men do things because they do those others. The nature of the causality remains another question, but the connections observed must first be stated (Arensberg and Kimball 1940:xxii–xxiii).

This was, I think, a good statement for its time, and remains so. Goddard had arranged the meeting in hopes of clarifying what we were doing. But there was no communication going on. After the silence had gone on for as long as I could stand it, I asked a question. I was scared to death, of course. I was a beginning graduate student, and this was seven years before I had a doctorate. But I had done some reading, which I'll come to in a minute, and on the basis of that, I asked Malinowski a question. I asked him if he meant it when he said that every thing, every item in culture, had a vital function – had to have a vital function. He said, "Yes." Now, that's where my hat comes into the story. I said to him, "In the back of my hat there is a little bow which is sewn on to where the seam comes. Now if you go to a store and try to buy a hat, you'll find it has that little bow in it." I asked him what its function was. There was some special reading I had happened to have done which made me know something about this, which I'll come to in a minute. But the binding of the hat is sewn together at the back end very tightly; the bow doesn't hold anything. If it isn't there, nothing will happen. Yet if you should happen to buy such a hat in a store, and it didn't have the bow, the salesman would say, "Wait a minute, I'll have the bow put on,'' and you'd get one with a bow. But, what function does it have? Well, Malinowski looked at it and said, "Well . . . " He thought first of course that maybe it held the hat together, and I showed him it didn't. So then he said, "Well, maybe it's decorative." I said, "How? You can't even see it." We went on like this, for some time, but he finally said, "Oh, I'm interested in important matters." He simply dropped it.

Now, where did I get this item, and what does it signify? I happened to be indexing the first forty volumes of the *Journal of American Folklore* – that's how I was earning my way through Columbia, for fifty cents an hour. If you start trying to index a thing like that – you know, you've got to have the title, you've got to have the author, and so forth, and maybe some subject questions and so forth – believe me, as you go through a volume and you put everything into an index, it becomes damned boring. So every once in a while, you say: "Oh, what the hell, at fifty cents an hour I'll read a paper." So you read an occasional paper instead of just indexing it.

And there were several papers in the early volumes of the *Journal of Folklore* by a man named Garrick Mallery.[9] He was an American ethnologist, and in these papers he was particularly interested in survivals, a theme made famous by Edward B. Tylor, who showed the important relation between survivals in culture, especially in children's games, and former ceremonies and rituals. Mallery took up this theme in his studies. In regard to the hat bow, his explanation was that this was a survival of something which had once been much more functional. At the back end of the hat ribbons were attached, and one wore the hat with ribbon streamers; style had gradually dictated that these become smaller and smaller, until they finally were stuck up inside the hat, and disappeared into the bow. So much for hats and Malinowski.

Five years later, Malinowski came to this country. He was invited to take over the graduate seminar in the Department of Anthropology at Columbia. When he took it over, he decided – or he was asked – to use the method that he used in teaching in England, which was what he called the Socratic method. He would ask a question, he would get an answer, he would tear the answer apart, and ask another question on the basis of the tearing; then you were supposed to fight back, then he would fight back and so forth.

Whoever gave him the list of people to call on must have hated my guts. When Malinowski started in, the first thing he did was to call my name. He asked me some question about kinship which had to do with the levirate and sororate, and I answered the question. He immediately disagreed with what I said, and repeated me is such a way that what he said I said was wrong. So I said, "I didn't say that." After a few corrections like this, he walked all the way down the room to see who he was talking to – because at that time, Malinowski was quite blind. At that point, he dropped his questioning, we had a few pleasant words, and he went back to the front of the room and called on someone else. At the end of the class, I went up to him and I said, "I wanted to greet you, because we met once before." He said, "I remember; we talked about hats."

But you see, stories aside, the problem presented by this, the problem of survivals in an historical view – of the way culture goes on, the persistences, sometimes for a century or more, of very meaningless features of design – I don't see how you escape its significance. His statement in that sense of functionalism, which would also be true of Radcliffe-Brown, was as erroneous as ever. I mention this by way of introduction; that's how I first met Malinowski. Now, we come to the year in which I gave the paper called "Functionalism in social anthropology." It was delivered in 1934, and published in 1935. I gave the paper for certain reasons. I am pretty sure that Radcliffe-Brown had not yet settled down in the United States. It was at a meeting of the American Anthropological Association. I thought I was posing certain objections in my paper to the work of some American ethnologists. I thought I was objecting to the kind of scholars whom I talked with at Columbia, Chicago and California, who were interested at the time in the kinds of things that Kroeber and Wissler and Spier were doing by way of historical reconstruction. If you've ever looked at the American Museum of Natural History volumes on age societies on the Plains or the attempts to reconstruct the history of the Sun Dance – well, this was the kind of history that was being done, and I didn't think it was historical.

At the same time, Ruth Benedict's book, *Patterns of Culture,* had focused people's attention on interrelationships within culture, and particularly in relation to the guiding motives that affect the life drives of people in a society, and through which you might try to understand the meaning or function of cultural forms. There had developed a kind of choice: "What do you do: historical studies or functional studies?" The functional studies were those of Margaret Mead, say, or Ruth Benedict. And the ones that were à la Ruth Benedict were, whatever else they professed to be, non-historical.

Fo example, let's take Zuñi, which is one of the peoples described in her book. The first Spanish influence in that area came with the Coronado expedition in 1540; and Benedict's research was done in the 1920s. During that time, all those Pueblos, especially the Eastern Pueblos, had been under the domination and control of Spanish military power, the pressure of the priests of the Catholic Church, missionaries, and all sorts of other pressures, including the economic pressures of Spanish trade and other trade. This had been going on irregularly since 1540. Now, one of the characteristic things that was said of the Pueblos in 1925 was that it was very difficult to work there because the people wouldn't trust you –

they wouldn't trust any white person, they wouldn't talk to any white person. Everything they did was secret; nobody could get into a *kiva* (ceremonial underground room). If you stop and ask yourself why this was so, you couldn't avoid remembering the long history of brutality, and of necessary distrust, that must have helped to preserve Pueblo cultures.

Dobu is another case. When Mead wrote, it had a population which was at most ten or twelve percent of what the population had been when Reo Fortune had studied them. What possible evidence is there that the institutions he had earlier described would have been the same as they were when the population was at its full size once the population had dwindled to twelve percent of its original size? We don't know – but it isn't discussed in Benedict or in Fortune.

The third case is the Kwakiutl of the Northwest Coast. Boas described them, and said that in the system of classes on the Northwest Coast, depopulation had been so serious that every Kwakiutl man could look forward to getting an honorific title and a position of prestige, because there were now more positions of prestige than there were men. Now, it was at that point that the descriptions that Benedict uses were secured. Boas didn't know – and I don't see how Benedict could have known – what was going on in Kwakiutl culture when there really were class differences, and when the population was at its height.

These are just illustrations of the way in which the configuration or patterning of culture was described by Benedict without regard to the historical context in which it occurred. With these sorts of things in mind, I was thinking that most of the people hearing my paper would be doing either studies in ethnology of the kind that Benedict emphasized, or else they would be doing reconstructions, à la Spier and Kroeber. Neither such approach coincided with my own thinking about this.

I had no knowledge, of course, that anybody but American ethnologists would be present at those meetings. But, at the end of my paper, Radcliffe-Brown stood up, and started to argue. His arguments went on to a point where I simply exited from the room, because he was arguing with everybody there, and they were answering him; I didn't have to say anything. As far as I could understand, there was a room full of people who agreed essentially with what I had been saying. I remember that before I left to talk to Sapir, William Duncan Strong not only argued for history and against Radcliffe-Brown, but quoted to Radcliffe-Brown from a review of my *Pawnee Ghost Dance Hand Game* which he had written giving it an unusually powerful recommendation. In particular, he quoted my assertion of "the inevitability of founding ethnological methodology on the metaphysic of history." He said that I had not only discussed the method from this point of view, but that I had published a study in which I had carried it out. After about forty-five or fifty minutes, when no real progress was being made in the discussion, it was suggested that since my paper was being published, Radcliffe-Brown should be invited to put together his response to my thesis, and to publish it in the same issue of the *American Anthropologist;* he agreed. That ended the discussion.

In the issue of the *American Anthropologist* in which our articles appeared, he wrote something that he did not republish when he later [1952] republished his paper. He wrote:

It has been suggested that the comments which I made on Dr. Lesser's paper when it was read at Pittsburgh should be printed to accompany it. It is unfortunate that Dr. Lesser, instead of specifying those who he regards as functionalist, and giving references to their works, offers us only an abstract description even while he himself indicates the lack of any unity amongst functionalists. Dr. Lesser assures me that he regards me as functionalist. I have never claimed the appellation, but it is true that I have made constant use of the concept of social function in lecturing and in writing since 1909. However, as will be seen, I do not define function in the same way as Dr. Lesser. In the circumstances, I cannot offer any real criticism to the paper. All that I can do is to offer for any interest it may have a statement of the way in which I myself apply the concept of function in the study of human society (Radcliffe-Brown 1935:394).

At that time, I accepted, as I still do, Arensberg and Kimball's description of the need to study the relationship among different aspects of a group's behavior, to find out the nature of such a relationship. I would never have dreamed of challenging Radcliffe-Brown on functionalism; all I was trying to do, I thought, was to talk sense about anthropology. Only much later did I begin to see the real point of my own paper. The discussion of function and of what is functional is secondary. The major importance of the paper was an attempt to elucidate what historical context means in understanding any situation.

From the time I entered anthropology, I was interested in finding regularities, or laws, of history, if possible. I had to use a concept of function which, as I stated it in the paper, implied a causal relationship. If you were going to stress the historical context in which a culture possessed its characteristic form or structure, the only way to do so scientifically would be to establish relationships that could be tested, or proved, to exist. The core of the paper deals with what history is, and the necessity of studying the kinds of functional relations I have described, if we are to discover regularities and laws. It also was meant to raise questions; since history is made basic to the argument, one must take into account relations through time, as well as relations at any one time (Lesser 1977).

This lengthy extract from Lesser's comments to a theory class represents one of the few records we possess of his informal teaching style: the assertive, humorous, impatient, and original manner in which he thought and taught. Another portion of the same record surfaces in the Introduction to Part III.

The second essay, "Problems versus subject matter as directives of research," is of a different sort. It was delivered as a paper in 1938 and published in the fall of 1939. By this time, Boas had retired, and the Second World War had just begun. In his essay, Lesser raises serious questions about the raison d'être of anthropology. Because he questions the scientific justification for anthropological research, he inevitably asks as well how such research may best be done, and to what ends and with what subjects. We anthropologists ought not, Lesser argues, defer to some indeterminate future our struggle to formulate and to solve problems of research or our obligation to test, and falsify if necessary, our own hypotheses. We cannot hide behind some abstract duty to collect more and ever more data. To justify our studies of "primitive" societies to the exclusion of other societies, Lesser says, we claim that a science of society "must be based upon data drawn from any and all societies of which there is or can be record, if it is to reflect that true range of facts and to reach generalizations of wide application and validity."

But then how can we be convincing, he asks, if we remain "endlessly curious about everything that has to do with man and his history and too consistently unwilling to set up our investigations in terms of decisive problems that can advance the science of society . . ."? Lesser considered his views consistent with Boas's own. Consistent they may have been, but my guess is that Boas might have found them distracting and even, perhaps, irrelevant. Lesser's pleas – for problems as against subject matter; for solutions as against cosmetic methodology; for a "more vigorous forming of inquiries" to "break down the artificial departmentalization of the social sciences" – were unusual for their time. His arguments were, in fact, startlingly modern, and it is remarkable that he advanced them nearly half a century ago.

3   Functionalism in social anthropology

The most vigorous tendency in social anthropology today is that of functionalism. To some the functional approach has seemed a radically new departure which invalidated earlier methods and interests; to others it has appeared a false doctrine, itself invalidated by already established technics. Several factors may be held accountable, however, for the fact that the issue between these antithetical reactions has not been clearly drawn.

The functionalist tends to assume that there exists, apart from functionalism, a homogeneous and unified subject matter, so that a disjunction can be made between functional social anthropology on the one hand and non- or pre-functional social anthropology on the other. Since as a matter of fact a considerable variety of methods and interests is to be found among non-functionalists, the functionalist often appears, from the standpoint of particular adversaries, to deny what is not asserted and to assert what is not denied.

The non-functionalist, motivated as he is at times by an understandable desire in the face of attack to hold fast to familiar ideas, often fails to distinguish the particular interests and conceptions of individual functionalists from the broader, more basic meaning of the functionalist approach. This confusion arises not only from the lack of unity among functionalists, but rests also upon a failure to differentiate content from method. Functionalists themselves are in part to blame for this ambiguity. Individual functionalists often concentrate upon the study of special phases of the subject matter and tend on occasion to identify the subject matter as such with these particular interests, and method with their particular procedure in handling a special subject. It is often not at all clear whether the functionalist is insisting upon the adoption of a certain method or the study of a certain subject.

This paper was read at joint sessions of the American Folk-Lore Society and Section H of the American Association for the Advancement of Science in 1934. It was published in the *American Anthropologist* 37:386–93. © 1935 the American Anthropological Association. Reproduced by permission. Not for further reproduction.

Clarity demands the discrimination of content and method. Scientific method as such is not limited in its application to any one phase of phenomena but can be applied wherever intellectual control of things is necessary. If functionalism involves a method which is of value in ethnology, it must be a mode of procedure which is independent of the particular use that has been made of it by functionalists.

Functionalists have not been alone in bringing to attention aspects of culture which in the past have been too much overlooked, but in particular they are responsible for the most part for the introduction into social anthropology, or in any case for the emphasis in social anthropology, of certain special types of cultural phenomena. Outstanding is, no doubt, the stressing of psychological aspects of culture. Factors in the molding of individual personality, conflict points in family and social life, dominant group or cultural attitudes, and the psychological root of institutional life, have been included in ethnological subject matter by various students. There has been a tendency also to emphasize the study of particular kinds of content more than others: sociological problems of aggregation and institutional function, economic institutions and their cultural roots, law in its basic relation to social life and culture, and, not the least of the emphases, detailed consideration of sexual life and education for the light they throw on fundamental differences of psychological patterns.

These suggestions, though obviously inadequate as a summary of functionalist interests, may serve for my purpose to indicate the way in which certain emphases in content have come into the subject matter of social anthropology along with functionalism. The question that concerns us is to what extent the ethnologist who is committed to functional method is committed to functional content.

The introduction of new emphases in content or interest must be expected in any field of inquiry. The growth and development of ideas in other fields is bound to produce a demand for comparable information such that a cross-fertilization will result. What has happened in social anthropology has obviously been that students have brought interests from other fields, notably psychology, sociology, economics, and law, and have worked ethnologically along the lines of these interests. All who share the conviction that social sciences are not water-tight compartments but merely the specialized treatments of different aspects of culture, must recognize that cooperative and collaborative effort between social scientists in different fields must be the dominant tendency if sound and unified social science is to result. Some of us, be it admitted, have felt that social sciences which have been limited to the phenomena of our culture alone have in the end more to learn from anthropology than social anthropology has to learn from these narrower disciplines. We have there-fore at times deplored the introduction from other disciplines into an-thropology of methods which seemed shaky and immature. Nevertheless, ultimate judgment of the value of approaching ethnological data from the standpoints of other social and psychological sciences must rest upon the pragmatic test. The enterprise will finally be judged in terms of its ac-complishment, and meanwhile, recognizing the difficulties inherent in these transfers of method, we must welcome the attempt.

But the fundamental question to which I return is whether the ethnol-ogist who values the functional approach must therefore adopt the content stressed by functionalists. Must the traditional ethnologist, who, for ex-ample, has been primarily interested in cultural structure – in social and religious life, in economics and material culture, in mythology and art – must that ethnologist put aside his own interests and assume that newer tendencies of method demand that he become psychologically minded and concern himself primarily with the patterning of attitudes?

It is my contention that there is no necessary connection between the essentials of functional method and the particulars of functional content. Subject to critical consideration, there seems much of value for the eth-nologist in the broad fundamentals of functionalism as a procedure. But the ethnologist must discriminate between particular functionalist claims and essential ideas. He may or may not adopt the interests of the func-tionalists, but he should adopt from them certain attitudes toward the study of culture and cultural problems. From this standpoint I should like to review briefly the antithesis between functional and non-functional approaches as regards fundamentals of method.

Functionalism, as any new movement in science, represents a reaction against doctrines felt to be outmoded. Functionalists have explained their own beginnings as determined primarily by an attempt to get away from the evolutionary conception of social history and from the so-called ev-olutionary comparative method. When this earlier view dominated in-vestigation, an observed cultural fact was seen not in terms of what it was at the time of observation but in terms of what it must stand for in reference to what had formerly been the case. Investigation brought out little of what the facts are and much of what the course of evolution was conceived to have been.

From the functionalist standpoint this earlier approach substituted theo-rizing for the discovery of facts. The reality of events, however, consisted of their manifestations in the present. Hence if events are to be understood it is their contemporary functioning which must be observed and recorded. The past as such is irrelevant, the present is primary. What is the case is what is seen to be the case here and now, and definition of process and function must be determined in phenomena as they are observed. The functionalist emphasizes the doctrine that investigation of customs and institutions must begin with their relation to immediate or contemporary conditions; he stresses the fallacy of assuming that remote factors are always more important than immediate conditions; and he tends toward the extreme of assuming that *only* contemporary conditions and factors are relevant.

That knowledge begins in the understanding of present experience is fundamental and unassailable. What is given is always contemporary experience, and it is true that knowledge of the past must necessarily be based upon contemporary events and processes. Since our experience in our own contemporary world is primary, and since our knowledge must be based upon it, the functionalist is correct in asserting that the primary subject of attention must be the present and contemporary functioning of things. This is true whether we are concerned with knowledge of the past or knowledge of the present. The archaeologist infers the past from remains found in the present, in terms of their relations to other factors known in the present. The past is always an inferential reconstruction drawn from present facts and conditions.

If we are concerned with the determinants of institutions and customs it follows that, whether in the end the determinants lie in past or in present conditions, procedure must begin by seeking explanation of the events first of all in present conditions and processes. Only when and insofar as the form being analyzed cannot be understood in terms of relations to other factors in the present, need we turn backward in time to find the past or former conditions which are major or relevant determinants. The procedure begins by using present conditions to define the determinants and relations of present events so far as that is possible, and then seeking factors more remote in time for the understanding of what is left unexplained by present conditions.

The fundamental question that concerns us here is in how far this turning backward to the past actually becomes necessary in practice. It is the tendency of the functionalist to deny that it ever does. What exists in the present has a present function, and to discover that function is the end of research. The functionalist often seems to assert that we must not only begin with the relations of cultural aspects in the present, but we must end there. Since history is merely inferred from present conditions, it is conceived irrelevant to the understanding of present conditions. This conception betrays a tendency to believe that knowledge based on inference is necessarily hypothetical and relatively uncertain. Inference, however, is a mode of thinking which is basic not only to the reconstruction of history, but to the derivation of functional relations in the present as well. Results that are based on inference are not as such theoretical or uncertain. The extent to which such results are to be accepted as valid and factual depends, both in the case of the establishment of functional relations and in the case of historical inferences, upon what the evidence is and what implications it supports.

The distrust of the functionalists for history derives in part from their distaste for evolutionary conceptions and their recognition that evolutionary ideas stemmed from historical interests. Evolutionary conceptions were embedded in nineteenth century historical tendencies in social science and human thought generally, and evolutionary anthropologists were no doubt historically minded when they set out to reconstruct a history of human culture and institutions. But is history to be impugned because of the errors in a particular conception of its nature?

Functionalists were not alone in their reaction against evolutionary methods. In point of fact they were anticipated in time by Franz Boas and the American school, and the reaction against evolutionary methods includes also the diffusionist approaches of English and German anthropologists. In the approach of the American school the point of departure was different. Evolution as a principle in social anthropology was attacked not because it was conceived as historical, but because it was shown by an appeal to the facts that it was not history. The critique was founded not on metaphysics but on an empirical investigation. The method called for a return to the study of cultures as such, insisted that hypotheses must spring from and be adjusted to the realities of cultural phenomena, and denied that cultural data could be deduced from and fitted to theories. The facts observed did not indicate that the course of human history had been what the evolutionists described. So much the worse for evolutionary conceptions. But evolution was never identified with history. Evolutionary doctrines were recognized to be deductive philosophies of history. Factual history was quite otherwise, and in attacking evolution, the American school did not impugn the significance of valid history, but on the contrary found that valid history was instrumental to adequate cultural understanding.

The American position is associated with a definite conception of history. The processes which control events lie embedded in time as well as place, hence the determining conditions and the associations and connections of events are in the past as much as (if not more than) in the present. From the standpoint of the time at which any event is viewed, we are dealing with a temporal cross-section of a continuum of events in time, and any aspect to which attention is directed is an end-point of continuing change, an end-point of the historic process. Hence while investigation must begin with what is the case in the present, it cannot end there. It is impossible to disregard the existence of a past because the career in time of anything or any event is more than momentary, and its nature and characteristics must be understood in terms of its relations to other events and things regardless of temporal limitations.

Justice demands that extremist tendencies of the American school be also kept in mind. Affirming an emphasis in research upon exact historical fact, the American ethnologist too often assumes that the determination of what the facts are in temporal historical terms is not only the basis of empirical knowledge but the end of research. Thus, whereas the functionalist, annoyed at the results of false historical theorizing, turns away from history to limit himself strictly to the consideration of immediate conditions in the present and contemporary, the American ethnologist, starting from a factual critique of inaccurate deductive history, and attempting to replace it with sound history, has in so doing often limited himself too strictly to the consideration of remote temporal relations of the conditions and events of the present.

In short, both the functionalist school and the historical school have at times been guilty of special and narrow biases. Historical ethnologists have attempted to develop short-cut methods to history and historical reconstruction, which short-cut methods are not only open to question as empirical methodologies, but which can in any case result only in the reconstruction of mere chronology in time of unrelated events. History cannot be identified with such mechanical reconstructions.

Functionalists, on the other hand, have too often identified the investigation of particular questions and the study of specialized aspects of the subject matter with correctness of method and content, and are too ready to identify history with bad history.

But apart from such confusions and occasional short-sightedness, there are at the root of both approaches certain sound and unassailable methodological assertions. Both have affirmed the necessity of a return to the study of cultural facts as they are found living and functioning in the present; both have insisted that customs and institutions be investigated in relation to their contexts and not apart from them. Cultural functions and functioning in the minds of the functionalists is no different in kind from the familiar emphasis of American ethnologists upon the necessity of studying the interrelationship of the aspects of culture.

The extremes toward which these apparently divergent doctrines tend point the moral of sound method. On the one hand, the functionalist, insisting upon founding his functional statements upon immediate relations in the present, is too blind to the fact that determining and fundamental relations only too often lie beyond the present in the past. And, on the other hand, the historically minded ethnologist is too ready to seek remote historical relationships and overlook others nearer at hand. Obviously, it is true that the first consideration must be of the context of cultural phenomena in the present, and it is also true that for the most part determinations of events in the present lie in the past. In beginning with present conditions, exact understanding of any particular institution or custom demands not only the calculation of its apparent connections in the present, but even more a recourse to the past, *so far as it is relevant* to the particular inquiry, for an understanding of the determining relationships which lie behind the event.

In its logical essentials, what is a functional relation? Is it any different in kind from functional relations in other fields of science? I think not. A genuinely functional relation is one which is established between two or more terms or variables such that it can be asserted that under certain defined conditions (which form one term of the relation) certain determined expressions of those conditions (which is the other term of the relation) are observed. The functional relation or relations asserted of any delimited aspect of culture must be such as explain the nature and character of the delimited aspect under defined conditions.

How are such functional relations to be established? First of all, we begin, as in any science, with observation. We see such and such events going on. Many things are always happening at the same time, however. How are we to determine whether or not those things which happen at the same time are related to one another? For it is obvious that they may be contemporary events, or even serial events, not because they are related to one another but because their determinants, unknown and unobserved, have caused them to happen at the same or subsequent times. In short, contemporary or associated events may be merely coexistences. Culture, at any one time, is first and foremost a mass of coexistent events. If we are to attempt to define relationships between such events it is impossible in view of the known historicity of things, to assume that the relations lie on the contemporary surface of events. Whatever occurs is determined more by events which happened prior to the occasion in question than by what can be observed contemporaneously with it. As soon as we turn to prior events for an understanding of events observed, we are turning to history. History is no more than that. It is a utilization of the conditioning fact of historicity for the elucidation of seen events.

There is, however, a further difficulty. Just as it is impossible to assume, or to derive by intuitional methods, the functional relations of things in the present, so by turning backward to the past it is impossible by mere inspection to find the significant relationships of past to present events. The required methodology is more complicated than that. It demands the consideration of all alternatives, and for exact determination of relevant relationships it calls for the comparison of many instances. Generic and fundamental relationships must be rigorously defined so that it can be asserted of them that these were the actually related conditions of the seen phenomenon, and that this was the phenomenal expression of those conditions and not any other.

The determination of such relationships *is* the definition of cultural functions and is inescapable if ethnological method is to be scientific. The *conditions* which functional investigation must take account of can be generalized as historicity – the fact that institutions, customs, beliefs, artifacts, have careers in time, and that their form and character is molded more by what has happened to them in the course of that history than by what particular things they occur associated with at any one time. Progressive method in social anthropology must increasingly eschew narrow biases and limitations and must approach the study of culture in terms of a functional historicity.

But the conception of functional historicity does not predetermine the content of subject matter. Content is determined by problems selected for treatment. Given a certain problem, the investigator carves out of the whole a relevant subject matter which includes his necessary data. What problems are to be attacked, and hence what subject matters are to be emphasized, will be determined at any time by the interests and training of the investigator and by considerations of the relevance of ethnological subject matter to broad questions of interests both inside and outside of ethnology. It is not only the problems and content stressed by the functionalists which can be handled in terms of a functional historicity. Whatever problems the ethnologist finds of importance can and should be so treated, including not only psychological and socio-psychological problems, but also the familiar questions of musical style, mechanical principles in material culture, form and style in art and artifacts, the structures of institutions and beliefs, etc., and even the historical reconstruction of the past itself – that primary bugaboo of the functionalist. For why should there not be a reconstruction of the past which takes account of the functional and significant relations of events?

The suggestions I offer imply no radical departure. Functional historicity calls only for a realization of the necessity of defining the functional or significant relations in culture – without which scientific knowledge is impossible – and of accepting as a basic condition the historicity of things.

4   Problems versus subject matter as directives of research

We have been asked to comment on recent ethnological theory and method. I propose to discuss one phase of recent work, the tendency, as yet perhaps in its inception, to stress problems rather than expansion of subject matter as directives of research. I think this the most important methodological tendency of recent years, and one which bids fair, if carried through consistently, to overcome many continuing difficulties and disagreements about the nature and content of social anthropology. For I think the failure to begin research with clear-cut and explicit statements of problems is responsible, at least in part, for the lack of a consistent development of our subject matter, for the continuing disagreement as to whether functional or historical interests should dominate our work, for attempts to separate theory and interpretation from fact, for the persistence of merely descriptive work, and for some of the difficulty which social scientists in other fields find in orienting themselves on what we have to say.

While a tendency is appearing to stress problems as points of departure, the implications of that method are not as yet carried out with any consistency. And the general tendency, as illustrated by field research in ethnology, is still along opposite lines. It is still a fact that most of our research is oriented around subject matter and not explicit problems. The field worker usually goes to a place, that is, a tribe, a cultural group, or an area, to bring back a general assortment of data about it, as well rounded as possible, which can be presented as a descriptive treatment of a people or a culture. The area or group is generally selected in terms of certain factors: first, that it has not been studied, or is not being studied by someone else at the time; second, that research money is available, ticketed for such areas or groups; third, that less is known about it than

This paper was read in the symposium on Recent Ethnological Theory at the Annual Meetings of the American Anthropological Association, New York, December 27, 1938. It was originally published in the *American Anthropologist* 41:574–82. © 1939 The American Anthropological Association. Reproduced by permission. Not for further reproduction.

other groups or areas, hence data will be helpful in filling out gaps in our descriptive knowledge. Insofar as a problem or problems are considered, it is usually assumed that they will be discovered in the material while in the field, or after returning from the field. Ordinarily, unless a dissertation is to come from the work, the written treatment which is presented is arranged around systematic description as a form, and the problems which may be amenable to treatment with the material, the questions which it might answer or settle, are treated incidentally, or left to later research by others, who, it is assumed, will use the monograph as a source.

Unfortunately, there is at the same time a tendency to feel that research in ethnology means field research primarily, and as a general rule today few problems are being attacked and settled on the basis of already recorded materials. Hence, in general, the investigation of the problems which the monograph might settle is not only postponed, but frequently postponed indefinitely.

Furthermore, where research is done in terms of recorded materials, rather than field work, it too labors under the handicap of beginning study and investigation, not in terms of problems, but of subjects. It is considered sufficient that a general interest is present in some phase of art, or music, or social organization, or religion, and the subject is studied. Problems are again postponed, and it is again assumed that in the course of studying the subject of interest, problems will raise their heads and will then be answered.

This may seem too extreme a picture, but it is true to too great an extent. And while problems of one sort or another always can be found in material, the question that needs to be asked is, are these the critical problems which we, at this stage of anthropological knowledge, need to settle and clear up, if we are to proceed vigorously and fruitfully? Or are these merely the problems which we have turned to by chance, regardless of their relevance to basic issues, regardless of their significance for others, because our material happened to lead us in their direction?

I think we can attribute to this research tendency some of the disapprobation felt among other social scientists for the ethnologists' continuing interest in primitives. For if a study is to be essentially descriptive, and is to take up only those questions which as a descriptive inquiry it itself suggests, what justification is there for studying primitive conditions rather than modern conditions? "Cultural relativity, the importance of cultural or social context, is already fully realized," such critics may say. "We recognize with you, and are happy to give you credit for making clear to us, the tremendous variation in patterning of social institutions and behavior, but, bearing that in mind, why not turn now to problems of contemporary civilization and make the point of view fruitful? And after all, if the application of knowledge to the solution of problems is to be regularly postponed until after data are secured by means of descriptive methods, why not at least deal analytically with modern civilization, where the future for application is not so far removed, since the data we will be considering are closely related to our own life and time?''

Ordinarily, we reply by restating our basic theme: that a science of society, if it is to be built, must be based upon data drawn from any and all societies of which there is or can be record, if it is to reflect the true range of facts and to reach generalizations of wide application and validity. But while we may be convinced of the correctness of our point of view, I confess that I do not see how it can carry conviction to others while we apparently remain a group of investigators endlessly curious about everything that has to do with man and his history and too consistently unwilling to set up our investigations in terms of decisive problems that can advance the science of society every time that a thorough piece of research is carried out.

I venture that at this point I must myself become more explicit as to what is meant by a problem, and in what way clear statements of problems will avoid so many false issues.

What is a genuine problem for scientific investigation? A genuine problem seems to be first of all the asking of a question, and the question must be put in such a form that it is possible, by referring to some body of fact or data, to reach a decision upon it, positive or negative. As a question, a problem does not arise in a vacuum, but is always connected with questions which were asked before and which have been answered positively or negatively. A problem therefore always postulates something, that is, it either raises a doubt and begins a denial of something which has been believed or affirmed, or it suggests a truth and begins an affirmation of something which has been doubted or denied. In this sense a genuine problem is a hypothesis which can be stated in an explicit form. One or two illustrations may make my meaning clearer. If we ask, is suicide a universal type of human behavior, that is, does it occur under any and every pattern of social life?, we ask that question because we have reason to doubt its universality, and are ready to put the problem to an empirical test. What is not doubted needs to call belief in question. If we say, individual ownership of land does not occur under hunting conditions of life where the chase, and not trapping, is the form of technology employed, we assert a potential truth, based on a functional consideration of the relations of technology to land ownership in one or more cases, which remains a hypothesis until we have put it to more complete testing and verification.

Problems then are hypotheses fundamentally. They assert something about the nature of the real world which is to be checked against the facts. As hypotheses, they are obviously drawn from prior investigation and research. Work already done suggests probable truths to be tested and probable falsehoods to be tracked down. In drawing upon past work in this way, the hypothesis links what has been done with what needs to be done. The more clearly such hypotheses are expressed, the more rapidly inquiry can move forward in fruitful directions.

At the same time, the clear formulation of hypotheses outlines as nothing else can the background of the known. The hypothesis frames what we expect to be true on the basis of past study and checks it in future study. Hypotheses of this character will differ in the degree of their probability. Some may prove immature guesses and intuitions which the facts rapidly disprove; others will be regularly sustained. There is no difference of kind between hypotheses and scientific laws, only a difference in degree of probability, affected by the extent to which verification has been found, and the extent to which we have reason to trust the sample of experimental tests which have been carried out. Hence, clear formulation of hypotheses in every research procedure leads in the direction of a recognition of the laws on invariant relations which may exist in our subject matter. For such laws are merely the statements of the normal expectations which we carry forward from one research performance to another. As any laws of science, they are subject to continual reverification, for any evidence which casts doubt upon them leads to a specific experimental test.

This view of problems as the necessary point of departure for research does not mean that the problems with which research is initiated will predetermine or pervert its outcome. Nor does it mean that problems will not arise in the course of the investigation. Nor that conclusions may not be exactly the opposite of what was expected, or at any rate, something very different. If we examine what we actually do in carrying through the investigation of a problem, these difficulties do not arise.

We begin with a hypothesis or hypotheses explicitly formulated, *and* with a body of more accepted beliefs which are not at the time subject to doubt. The facts may prove the hypothesis wrong, and we may have to accept its opposite as true. Or the facts may make it necessary for us to amend or qualify the hypothesis so that we thereafter assert its truth only under certain more limited conditions. Meanwhile, as we deal with the facts some normal expectation or belief of ours which we had not expected to find challenged may become doubtful. Some special type of novel information or condition comes to light. We then take on the additional problem of rechecking or verifying something which we had considered a foregone conclusion, and perhaps correcting it. Genuine problems of the nature of hypotheses which develop in the course of investigations – and are usually put down merely to the fact that they *come out* of subject matter – are essentially of this kind. They flow from the discovery that what we expected to be the case has in some way proved inaccurate, and at that point a crucial question of major importance develops. Hence we do not have to fear that clear statements of problems beforehand will blind us to problems that may turn up in the course of inquiry. On the contrary it is likely to lead us more directly to the crucial problems which may exist in the particular phase of data upon which we work. And it *leads* us to them, for the most part, instead of allowing us to stumble upon them by chance. As a result, the problems which will be tackled at the beginning and during research will regularly be vital to the whole subject matter.

From this standpoint, it is worth considering whether it is ever true that we can merely approach subject matter for study, without problems being involved or hypotheses assumed. When, for example, we are dealing with what purports to be merely a study of the distribution of some institution or trait, is *no* problem involved, or is the problem merely left inexplicit? Thus, are we not really gathering data which, if it answers any questions at all, answers certain broad amorphous questions about cultural imitation and adaptation? If we try to make explicit what a merely distributional study can answer, I think we will find that they are questions we know the answers to only too well already. It is for that reason that cultural distributions cannot be fruitfully carried out as research problems, at least from this point of view. It is when a genuine problem requires, as part of the facts relevant to its specific solution, knowledge about the distribution of some cultural aspect in space or time, that charting the distribution becomes a means to an end and as such not only significant and valuable but indispensable.

A mere distribution study does not avoid problems, it merely leaves them inexplicit, and making them explicit would in many cases show the problems to be sterile. At the same time it does not escape having made assumptions, although the hypotheses too are left unstated. For a distribution study assumes certain truths about cultural borrowing or diffusion; it is based upon certain expectations that have grown up in the course of prior investigations.

I have chosen the illustration of distribution studies, partly because it illustrates my theme directly, partly because it is a familiar phase of our work. But I think what it shows is true of many types of general study of subject matter which do not take a clear point of departure in problems explicitly stated. We run the risk in such cases that we may not be settling issues of any importance at all, but merely rehandling old themes. There was a time, for example, when distribution studies were crucial experiments. When it was generally believed that institutions arose essentially by evolving from earlier institutional forms as a result of factors which were inherent in the earlier form, it was experimentally necessary to show by distribution studies of myths and tales, of men's societies, of rituals, of the use of pottery, and so on, that fundamental similarities occurred within contiguous territories in a great many cases and were not found outside these areas, in order to prove that borrowing was the process which explained them and that therefore outer factors as well as inner factors have been fundamental in the development of the cultural situation found in any one time and place. Distribution studies were in this earlier connection a means to an experimental end. At the same time they brought into the field of our subject matter many facts of distribution. As a result, if subject matter rather than problems is the point of departure, there is a tendency to be tantalized by the many distributions still awaiting cartography. But I think we have to ask whether the possible distribution studies which can be made are not infinite in number, and whether therefore any specific study should not be carried out when it is a vital means to an experimental end, and not merely upon its own account.

Clear formulation of problems can guard against turning a technical means of investigation into an end in itself. For there is always the need for perfecting our techniques, the means by which we investigate and collate data for the solution of problems, but unless the major problems are borne constantly in mind, there is always the danger that attention may be drawn too completely into the merely technical questions of perfecting means of getting at facts and too completely away from the fundamental questions which make those facts meaningful and important. The archeologist as well as the descriptive ethnologist needs I think to guard against this type of technical absorption, and can do so by orienting research from basic and fundamental problems.

This view, illustrated by distribution studies, can, and I think – though it seem heresy – *should* be applied to the question of field research in various areas and among various peoples of the world. There was a time when so little was known about primitive areas and groups, and so much was asserted, that every investigation cast a halo of doubt around most of the statements which had been made about primitive mankind. It became necessary therefore to sample, as rapidly and as extensively as possible, the cultures and social institutions of the primitive world. Every culture threw a flood of light upon our whole view of mankind and human behavior. But today another merely descriptive treatment of another primitive group can serve no such eloquent function. Witness the eagerness with which the research student tries hopefully to find a culture or a people from whose ways of life he can, in a merely descriptive way, report something spectacular. The escape from this situation can come only when we realize that clearly formulated experimental problems must take us to the region and the culture, not a general interest in field work. The culture or group should be selected, regardless of whether it is well known or badly known, near or far, because we have explicit hypotheses in mind which we have reason to believe can be settled by an appeal to the facts in such a specific case or cases.

Such heresy may lead to the fear that, as we have often expressed it in the past, many primitive cultures and groups may die out under our very eyes before we get to them. Yes, they may. And they also do, in spite of our fears and worries. First of all, I think we need to recognize that the description of every human culture and group of every time and place in the whole history of mankind is an actual impossibility. While we attempt it, every culture which we thought we had described has changed and become quite different. We cannot capture time in some static framework and hold it still. We will always be limited to a sample of the cultures and societies which have existed or exist. The real question is whether the sample which we have and shall have will have been determined by the chance of miscellaneous curiosity, or by intelligent selection along the lines of crucial problems. For an approach to the field in terms of problems will not mean less field work; it may well mean more. But it will necessarily mean that the selection of cases which become available will have been determined by genuine questions which exist and which it is of importance to answer. Nor can we fall back upon the ready answer that today we should merely report, because the future will have different questions to answer. We cannot know those questions today and therefore cannot anticipate what data will be necessary to answer them. But future inquiries must in any case stem from present work. If present effort is directed toward the ordered investigation of problems and the collection of data relevant to them, and if we chart the further course of investigation through clear-cut hypotheses, the future problems will develop in an orderly manner out of present problems, rather than out of a mere miscellany of fact and inquiry. And if they do so develop out of well-conceived programs of inquiry, the data which we collect along lines of problems will inevitably prove more relevant and fruitful than the merely miscellaneous could possibly be. And of course there will always be human cultures or human culture, at least so long as there are ethnologists. So that, though some questions may arise that we cannot have the answers to, most genuine problems will prove capable of an empirical solution in terms of available materials. And there are likely to be some problems in the future on which we lack the facts we would like to have no matter what methods we use today in carrying forward field research.

A research orientation through problems seems to make the apparent issue between functionally and historically minded bitter-enders an unreal one. If hypotheses are clearly stated, and if they derive from the known and ask the further questions that need to be asked, it is obvious that the investigator must turn to the data with one fundamental criterion in mind – what is relevant to the solution of this problem? He cannot say he will deal with one kind of fact or another. Some facts may lie in the contemporary dimension, others in the historical. It is a rare, perhaps an impossible case that all relevant facts should lie exclusively in one plane or the other. With relevance as his guide, the investigator needs to take one special caution from the historical nature of his facts, from their condition of historicity. He can investigate far enough, in terms of possibilities, to find out all relevant functional facts which exist in the *present*, but some functional connections with the *past* may be impossible to discover. The investigator must therefore, in relation to his problem, calculate what the alternative possibilities of this historical phase may be, and must so frame his conclusions or further hypotheses that they cannot be invalidated by the later discovery that one *or* the other of the historical possibilities is actually the case, but remain true no matter what the as yet unknown historical factors eventually prove to be. It is this limitation of historicity which is fundamental, not a crude need for historical reconstruction in relation to any and every problem. If some history is irrelevant, it should be left so. But what may prove relevant and is unknown must be taken into account or conclusions are unnecessarily shaky.

The statement of hypotheses explicitly can also serve to obviate the need so often felt for separating theory and interpretation from fact. To the extent that any gathering of facts, that is, any attention to subject matter, begs the question of hypotheses and problems merely by leaving them inexplicit, it is highly questionable whether such a separation is actually possible. What may be meant when this dichotomy is asserted is that fancy-free speculation is being avoided. But perhaps a better way to avoid loose speculation is to make our actual speculations into definable statements of what we are inquiring into and why on the basis of the data already in hand we have certain expectations. When we do so our theory and our empirical work go hand in hand. We need no apology for such theory inasmuch as if we retain it, it will be because the facts have warranted our claiming it as a verified hypothesis.

The increasingly contemporary question of the relation of anthropological data and methods to allied fields of the social sciences would be clarified if more of our research were approached from a problem point of view. Recognizing as we do the relevance of facts from many cultures rather than from one to the solution of problems faced by the psychologist, economist, sociologist, and political scientist, a more vigorous framing of inquiries would rapidly break down the artificial departmentalization of the social sciences, and prove to all social scientists that problems of human behavior must be followed through integrally regardless of the traditional boundaries of specialization. We can, I believe, look forward to the existence of a science of society as central and fundamental in a day when the nice discriminations of here and now as to exactly what is psychological and not sociological, what sociological and not economic, etc., are forgotten. In the development of such a science of society social anthropology can and must play a vital role, because it is in the nature of the primitive material with which we in particular deal that the degree of social and institutional differentiation so true of modern society is not found, and within which therefore we do not find the social, economic, political, psychological, religious, and so on, nicely discriminated but rather pooled in an intricate interplay. But to make this contribution to modern social science it seems to me that we must become increasingly aware of the problems we carry forward and transform them into explicit hypotheses in terms of which we direct our research. This is not easy. It is far simpler to turn to descriptive material with a general curiosity and interest and let what may come come, than to do the hard work of thinking out in advance what is known and what needs to be checked and made known. But difficult as the task of defining our problems and hypotheses may be, and thankless as it occasionally may prove when some fond hypothesis proves a dud, it seems to me that it is the price we must pay if we are to make any rapid progress toward the solution of genuine problems of social and human importance with which we can deal in a changing world and toward the development of a rigorous science of society.

Part III

Evolution

Introduction to Part III

More of Alexander Lesser's thinking about social and cultural evolution surfaces in the preceding essays than it does in the two that follow, which address the theory of evolution directly. The first, "Evolution in social anthropology," was delivered as a paper at a meeting of the American Anthropological Association in 1939, but was not published until 1952, thirteen years later, with the following comment: "The text was lost for a good many years. It is offered now, as given in 1939, because of the greatly increased interest in the subject that has developed during the intervening years, and because a good many personal inquiries about the paper have led the author to believe that its publication, even unchanged, may still be useful in 1952."

It seems to me that this paper marks a definite break with so-called Boasianism, but Lesser would probably never have agreed. Because of Boas's enormous influence in American anthropology and his distrust of social evolutionary theory, anthropological evolutionists were few and far between in the United States as they were nearly everywhere else. Writing in 1941, only shortly before his death, Bronislaw Malinowski took note of the rate attention evolutionary theory received in the United States at the time, but he concluded that "It has been revived in this country in a rational form by several young students, notably A. Lesser and L. White" (Malinowski 1944:17). Julian Steward, perhaps the most important U.S. anthropological evolutionist of this century, also repeatedly referred to Lesser's work. In an article on cause and regularities in culture, Steward noted that "even some members of the so-called 'Boas School' expressly advocate a search for regularities," and cited Lesser's early papers (Steward 1949:2). As I suggested in the Introduction to Part I, Lesser wanted to demonstrate that Boas was not antievolutionary; but in the two papers reprinted here it is Lesser, not Boas, who seeks to ground social evolutionary theory in a scientific anthropology.

The second paper, "Social fields and the evolution of society," appeared in 1961 (nine years after the publication of the "evolution" essay,

73

but actually twenty-two years after that paper was written). During the same classroom session on theory I cited in the Introduction to Part II, Lesser commented on what led him to write the "social fields" paper:

An early influence in my ethnological studies was a book by G. C. Wheeler, called *The Tribe and Intertribal Relations in Australia* (1910). Wheeler explained that in Australia there was feud, vengeance, and conflict – but there was no war. It was news to many people, and I'm sorry to say it's probably still news to a lot. The facts Wheeler presented were accurate; the relationships between any local group and other groups around it were such that there was no such thing as an isolated separate horde in Australia. That no one seemed to want to recognize this lack of isolation bothered me.

I was troubled by the extent to which efforts were constantly made to disregard the relationships between and among social aggregates. I would get bored reading Plains ethnology, where you would find a footnote declaring: "The Cheyenne and the Arapaho were their traditional enemies, the Dakota their traditional friends." What does it mean? A series of studies that fill up five volumes, and there's this little footnote – and nothing else in any of the volumes about this assertion. What does it mean to be on friendly or unfriendly terms with another group? The relationships, after all, are the crux of things.

Again, take Malinowski's great work on the Trobriand Islanders. Malinowski got to the Islands by British ship; those ships were part of the administrative apparatus with which the British government ruled the Trobrianders. They used to take young men off the Islands for forced labor in other areas. If you've read Malinowski's *Myth and Primitive Psychology* (1926), he tells the story at one point concerning his discussions with the Trobrianders on the role of the male in conception. One Trobriander, to finish off an argument, said, "See that woman over there? Her husband has been working for six years at such-and-such an island; the British took him over. She has two babies; and he hasn't been back on a visit." Malinowski quotes this story; but never once does he discuss what effect on social structure, on social behavior, or on institutions, the taking away of a whole generation of young men to work on other islands has had. As far as he's concerned, it doesn't have any effect. He saw things the same way in Africa. Max Gluckman (1949) has explained how, in Malinowski's treatment of African society, he discusses each society without reference to the fact that its system of law and order, indirect rule, was completely controlled by the British representative, or that missionaries had been there working on the people for generations, or that they'd been deeply affected by trade and labor. Malinowski doesn't talk about that; he always talks about the pattern of native life as if these aspects don't exist. It was such omissions that led me to the considerations I deal with in this paper.

Robert Redfield was another exponent of the idea of isolation, and in his book, *The Little Community* (1955) he starts off with definitions of the little community. One of the basic points in the definitions is that the little community is separate, isolated, etc., and that's why you can study it so conveniently. Further on, Redfield discovers that there's no such thing as perfect isolation, but there are some communities that are very nearly isolated. Further on, he begins using cultural isolation in the sense of social distance from more active cultural centers. In *The Folk Culture of Yucatan* (1941), this view has led him to relate isolation specifically to the distance between each community and the capital: supposedly, the farther away it was, the more isolated it was. Distance from urban centers becomes a substitute for what was originally physical and social isolation. But later, he argues for something else which dominated his thinking about this for a long time, namely, that communities are best studied *as if* they were socially isolated, whether they are or not. This became his strongest argument in favor of the concept of isolation, but I submit that not one of these arguments was satisfactory.

Hunt's *The Wars of the Iroquois* (1940) makes my same point, though in a different way. He shows that the League of Iroquois didn't begin as the Deganaweda myth has it, with some individual standing up and organizing the League, but rather by social affiliation between the tribes. Stronger bonds of coordination and cooperation gradually evolved over a period of several centuries.

It was also influenced by V. G. Childe's *Social Evolution* (1951). Childe argues for the concept of social evolution, advanced also by [Leslie] White.[10] He shows that throughout Asia Minor, all sorts of trade was going on during an immensely long period, before and after the invention of agriculture and husbandry. He explains the development of the social division of labor in these areas, and he makes the distinction between intracommunal specialization – where there is specialization of activities and occupations within the community – and intercommunal specialization, where there are differences of activity and production between communities. It is the second which involves almost constant group trade. The important point here is the fundamental fact that trade, division of labor, and interrelation of communities is verified by the archeology of the early Neolithic. Much the same thing could be found in aboriginal Middle America. Trade was fundamental; the politics of conquest states was also involved.

It is impossible to talk about human societies as isolated. This was the old sociological view; indeed, I'm willing to admit that my dear teacher Franz Boas was wrong on this point, and [Ruth] Benedict followed Boas. Conflict was seen to occur because societies are closed, and they get into conflicts with other closed societies. But, there has to be a reason for so-called closure. Closure is not a natural consequence of the existence of society, but quite the contrary; the existence of society means social relationships. Whether they are broken off or whether they develop, it involves some kind of functional activity.

For instance, my Pawnee informants said that in the nineteenth century, peace between Plains tribes that had been in conflict was achieved as follows. At any time among the Pawnee, for example, some individuals in the group had friends in another group, if there were any friendly relations at all. Let us say that a few Pawnees had some friends among the Cheyenne, but that the Pawnee were not on friendly terms with the Arapaho. At regular intervals, some six or so Pawnees would want to visit their Cheyenne friends, and they did so by getting together packages of tobacco wrapped in hide; they would put these into a larger package, which was taken by messenger and given to one of the leading chiefs of the Cheyenne, who would accept it and distribute it to the six Cheyenne friends of the Pawnee. There would be other Pawnees who would also want Cheyenne friends, so there would be extra packages without specified recipients. If these packages were accepted, a couple of weeks later the six Pawnee friends would go with gifts and things to trade to visit their Cheyenne friends. Each was received by his own Cheyenne friend and stayed in his lodge. This involved some trade; later there would be a general gathering. At some later time, the Cheyenne friends would send tobacco back to the Pawnee. My informant said the Pawnee were not on friendly terms with the Arapaho; but the Cheyenne and Arapaho were virtually allies. If the Pawnee wanted to end a conflict between themselves and the Arapaho, they did it through their Cheyenne friends. When the right day came, the whole Pawnee group would come forward to greet the Arapaho, led by the six Cheyenne friends of the Pawnee. The two sets of friends brought the groups together. This shows how relationships between groups could operate.

So this paper takes the position that any wholesale ignoring of the basic relationships of people, of the universal instances of what we call borrowing and diffusion, is erroneous. Borrowing and diffusion happen over and over again, and are characteristic of human social relationships. It is impossible to discuss the social structure and activities of people in any social group without taking account of borrowing and diffusion.

If you take this view, you assume that there is no limit to the relationships of people in any group to other groups, particularly the relationships you find at the most simple level. These things influenced me to attempt to show that you had to take account of the context of relationships of any groups with other groups in understanding social behavior. Ultimately, it was the field of relationships, whatever those relationships were, with which you had to operate, if you were going to understand what was going on. Thirty years before, I'd said that the view of history as mere happenstance, which interferes with the analysis of social process and systems of relationships, would not do. History is not happenstance. History and synchronic analysis are both parts of one universal history. For what is synchronic that is not also diachronic? How do you explain anything diachronic without considering synchronic relations? On close examination, distinction becomes meaningless; it's as artificial as defining one area as the area under study, without a willingness to see its interconnections outside (Lesser 1977).

In an important work that integrates historically the growth of the modern Western world with those non-Western areas and peoples who then came to be defined in terms of it, Eric Wolf has noted how Lesser called into question the idea of fixed, impermeable, societal boundaries. Wolf argues that "the concept of the autonomous, self-regulating and self-justifying society and culture has trapped anthropology inside the bounds of its own definitions," and calls for a single, unified history of peoples and cultures. "These remarks," he adds, "echo those made by the anthropologist Alexander Lesser who, in a different context, asked years ago that 'we adopt as a working hypothesis the universality of human contact and influence'; that we think 'of human societies – prehistoric, primitive, or modern – not as closed systems, but as open systems'; that we see them 'as inextricably involved with other aggregates, near and far, in weblike, netlike connections'" (Wolf 1982:18,19). One reason why Lesser's contribution to this issue was substantial was because it involved him in dialogue with anthropologists whose general orientation resembled his own, but who were prepared to treat human social groupings as neatly bounded integers, available for easy statistical manipulation. Counting cases in order to establish statistical correlations is a valuable tool in all science; but Lesser's readiness to raise doubts about the anthropological units of analysis employed in such treatments was bold and imaginative.

5   Evolution in social anthropology

Social evolution, in the form given it by Morgan, Tylor, Spencer, and other "classical evolutionists," is today as dead as a doornail in social anthropology. None would maintain with Tylor that "institutions of men are as distinctly stratified as the earth on which he lives" and "succeed each other in series substantially uniform over the globe"; or with Morgan that all economic, social, and political institutions can be classified into exact stages of savagery, barbarism, and civilization, "connected with each other in a natural as well as necessary sequence of progress"; or would interpret cultural history with Spencer as part of a cosmic scheme of transition from incoherent homogeneity to coherent heterogeneity. As a result of a generation of forceful and detailed critical work, these, and any similarly absolute principles of cultural history, have been discarded from our methodology.

Nor are they likely to come back. For today, when social anthropology has come of age, theory can no longer be loose speculation, but must grow out of research done and have implications for research to come. If we are critical of the nihilistic tendencies of the anti-evolutionists, it is with no will to revive disproved evolutionary doctrines, nor yet in any failure to recognize that vigorous denunciation and even dogmatism may have been necessary at a time when the fascination of evolutionary speculation inhibited empirical research. If there are signs and portents today of a growing feeling that the critical period which Goldenweiser has called "the downfall of evolutionism" may have substituted dogmatic denial for dogmatic acceptance, it is rather because of an interest in the problem of cultural growth and development, and a conviction that the errors which have been made in the past in approaching that problem have not elim-

This paper was delivered at the December 1939 Annual Meetings of the American Anthropological Association with the title "The present status of evolution in social anthropology." It was published as "Evolution in social anthropology" in *Southwestern Journal of Anthropology* 8 (1952):134–46. Reproduced by permission of the *Journal of Anthropological Research* (formerly *SWJA*).

inated the problem. Those errors may instead have more clearly defined the problem for us, and the positive ways in which it can be attacked. The question that is being asked today is whether, when all the negative tenets of the anti-evolutionists have been taken into account, there is not left a theory of cultural development which is consistent with our factual discoveries and which has implications for our actual work in research.

To assess this possibility does not today jeopardize our methodology, and such an assessment can be approached in an objective spirit. We must first of all recognize the negative propositions about cultural development which have already been established, and the necessity that any positive view which is taken must accept their limitations.

What is commonly accepted as proved about the development of cultures and civilizations? First, cultural history is not a unilineal order of developmental stages. A serial development based on the history of a single area cannot be assumed to hold universally for all areas. If sequential developments are considered "evolutionary," there are, from this standpoint, evolution*s* and not *an* evolution.

The social orders in which events have happened are not necessary and inevitable. They do not constitute closed systems of cause and effect relations. At many points of any order of actual happenings, accidental interrelations of events, of a strictly historical and unpredictable character, have been the determining factors.

The influence of outer factors, as in the phenomena of cultural contact and diffusion, or in the conditions of geographical environment, prove that cultural development is not an "unfolding of the preformed." Determinants of a cultural situation were not inherent in some remote preceding condition. The earliest beginnings of which we have record are not inevitable starting points, as we see clearly in a comparison of the Paleolithic technology of Europe, with its consciousness of form, with that of China, with its consciousness of function. Future cultural events cannot be predicted as inevitable occurrences.

Developmental change in culture is not necessarily from simple to complex. Simplification may itself be a developmental change, as we see frequently in the morphology of languages. Primitivity may remain relatively stable, as proved by the existence of extremely simple societies among our primitive contemporaries. Secondary primitivity may occur as a result of historical and environmental factors which cause a loss of useful arts and techniques.

There are no transcendental scientific standards on which to base the idea that the changes which have happened in the history of civilization constitute an orderly moral progress, or contain within them some cosmic idea or purpose, or are the inevitable expression of human striving in some pre-ordained direction. We eschew all subjective judgment, and, along with it, the use of cultural history as a basis for social Darwinism. We do not tolerate as scientific the use of such conceptions as struggle for existence, natural selection, and survival of the fittest, as rationalizations of the existence of war, of slavery, of the inequities of any economic system, or of imperialistic exploitation of native peoples by the European.

In our detailed treatments of culture, we do not loosely accept similarities as parallels which indicate historical equivalence of development. We recognize that similarities of parallels may be convergent, or may prove diffused borrowings or merely superficial and incomplete functional equivalences. Nor do we interpret existing institutions as survivals until we have explored their functional meaning in contemporary cultural contexts. We find it impermissible to reconstruct hypothetical earlier conditions by mere inference from existing institutions. Insofar as we deal with historical sequences of earlier and later, we limit ourselves to facts and conditions known to exist through archeology, or through recorded descriptions of living cultures. And in the case of our surviving simplest peoples, we do not accept their present conditions as equivalent automatically in all particulars to the former condition of other more complex civilizations.

A further stricture has been developed mainly by the functionalists, viz., that it is impossible to understand the character and meaning of a present institution by an appeal to its origins. The basis for this view is the phenomenon which has been termed "emergence" by Lloyd Morgan, or "creative synthesis" by Wundt. A new structural interrelation which comes into being as a combination of structural parts which earlier existed independently of one another has a novel relational quality on its own account which neither results from, nor could have been predicted from, the qualities of its parts. Such emergent qualities must be explored on their own account in the context in which they function, to be understood.

It is in the sense of these negative propositions about culture history and process that social evolution has no standing in contemporary anthropology. Anthropologists today accept them; the classical evolutionists would have largely accepted their opposites. If cultural evolution or development is to have a meaning for social anthropology today it must first take into account such negative propositions as these.

The question being asked, however, is whether a conception of evolution must involve these discarded views, or whether it may not have a meaning distinct from such ideas and consistent with all the fundamental limitations on which we insist. In this connection, it is worth recalling that anthropologists who reject evolution in culture and society, and even taboo the use of the word, nevertheless affirm unequivocally the reality of evolution in biological forms. What is it that anthropologists, in common with other scientists, mean when they affirm biological evolution? Do they affirm what they deny of cultural process, or do they recognize a different use and reference of the conception and term? And if so, would a similar use be applicable to culture, and would it if so applied, aid the social anthropologist in his work?

Biologists do not agree about the mechanisms of evolutionary change, but they universally accept evolution as a historical fact. Darwin's phrase that there has been "descent with modification" is perhaps the simplest formulation of what there is agreement upon. Living forms are genetic descendants of earlier and extinct forms, and modification has occurred in the course of that history. Complex, differentiated forms, where they occur, are genetic descendants of simpler, more undifferentiated ancestors. Many forms which are today distinct, if not all living forms, are genetically related to one another through common ancestors, and have become different as a result of a long process of change and modification.

Biological evolution is so often thought of in relation to the problems of *mechanisms* of change, that we may underestimate the fundamental importance of the general fact of evolution in human thought, even in its naked and severely limited form. If we recall the alternative, the clarification contributed by the idea of descent with modification is clear. Before evolution, organic (and inorganic) origins were conceived in biblical terms. The world was some six thousand years old, and all the varied forms in it were distinct, unrelated species, each independently created by an act of divine will. As opposed to this, descent with modification expressed the fact that historically there had been continuity, that the present was continuous with the past as far back as we had evidence, that forms in the present were not of distinct independent origin but related through links in their ancestry, and that complex, functionally differentiated forms were not creations de novo but the end result of a long history of changes and could be traced back to earlier simpler forms in the past.

Change within continuity is the fundamental meaning of this view. It does not imply, and biologists would not assert as scientific principles, that the course of change was a unilineal development, or an inevitable and predictable serial order, or a realization of latent potentialities, or a necessary transition from simple to complex, or a progressive moral order. Biological evolution does not define a development from one-celled organisms to man in which all intermediate forms find some definite place in a single, ordered series of changes. On the contrary, many independent lines of development are recognized and explored, and, like the bird and man, are conceived as involving independent courses of historical change.

In the study of variation, mutation, or selection, an interaction of hereditary and environmental factors is taken into account. This in itself is a recognition of the role of historical accident. For the environment which comes in contact with the organism at any particular time is a result of an independent series of causal events. The interrelation of two systems of events, represented in the interaction between organism and environment at a particular time, is an accident which could not have been predicted from the standpoint of either series alone. Hence the variation or selection which occurs was not preordained and was not predictable. Although its causes can be understood, it was not fated to happen, but did occur historically in a certain way.

Since a particular form is a product of complex interactions of organism *and* environment, an evolutionary change cannot be an "unfolding of the preformed," that is, a result of factors inherent in the earlier organism alone. Environmental factors, as well as potentialities of the earlier organism, must be taken into account.

Complex forms are found to involve simpler ancestral origins, but biology does not claim that when change occurs it must be in the direction of greater complexity and differentiation. The continued existence of one-celled organisms is inescapable evidence that simplicity may persist without marked change. Phenomena of degeneration, illustrated strikingly in many parasitic forms of arthropods and coelenterates, proves that change, when it occurs, may go from relative differentiation and complexity in the direction of greater simplicity. Changes which happen must be understood historically in terms of complex interactions of organism and environment, and may develop from simple to complex, or the reverse.

Biological evolutionists do not predict what form will arise in the future. Present conditions show that forms are still plastic, in differing degrees, that tendencies may be observed in the changes going on, but the biologist limits his attention to the observation and record of events and the analysis of hereditary and environmental factors in change as it happens.

Clearly evolution as we affirm it of biological forms does not involve the meanings to which we take exception in our critical studies of the work of cultural evolutionists. We may ask, then, whether the limited meaning of evolution in biological forms, can be profitably used in relation to culture.

In culture, as in life forms, there has been descent with modification in the sense that there has been continuity, and change within the continuity. Present civilizations are historically continuous with past culture, as far back as we have evidence. No civilization has arisen as a spontaneous generation de novo, nor by act of a divine will. Cultures which are now distinct are linked historically by common origins in the past, from which divergence has taken place in the course of a long history of changes, as a result of many complex historical events and factors. Involved in the process are conditions of both isolation and contact, of borrowing and independent development. And where complex cultures and civilizations occur, we know that historically they involve cultural origins in simpler conditions. Simplicity and lack of differentiation may persist, relatively unaltered, as we see in the present existence of marginal cultures, like the Ona or Yahgan, the Andaman, the Australian, Pygmy, and so forth. Change, when it happens, need not result in greater differentiation and complexity, since we see the reverse process happen in what the Kulturkreis school calls "secondary primitivity," which may have occurred among some Vedda and Bushman groups. But, while we limit our view of cultural continuity and change by the principles that differentiation need not appear, that change may be from complex to simple as well as from simple to complex, that there is no one line of development through which changes must go when they happen, we can nevertheless affirm, unequivocally, that differentiated societies arise on a simpler base.

This view that a process of growth, accretion, specialization, and differentiation of function lies historically behind any advanced or complex form of civilization which occurs, forms an actual principle of our methodology. It is not an empty phrase, but expresses the way we work and the way we think. It can be illustrated strikingly in the historical work of the archaeologists. When an advanced civilization, like that of the Maya or Aztec, becomes known, the archaeologist looks for stratification under it which may yield horizons of greater primitivity and perhaps account in part at least for the growth of the advanced culture from simpler origins. When the archaic [archaeological period] of Mexico becomes known, simpler than the Mayan as it is, it is still not accepted as a primitive base because it involves arts and technologies which we implicitly recognize must themselves be explained by a historical process of growth and development. The whole question of whether the higher civilizations of Mexico and Central America arose in situ or were intrusive from other regions is involved in this principle of work. When diffusionists of the Elliot Smith school assert the origin of Mexican cultures outside the Americas and their importation across the Pacific, the archaeologist who attempts to prove them American developments must base his reply not merely on improbability, but upon a demonstration that the development of Mexican cultures from simpler origins can be understood in terms of factors to be found within the Americas, perhaps in the Central American regions themselves. In the same way we do not assert that the earliest culture known in the New World was intrusive from the Old merely because we have as yet no evidence of an antiquity as great as that known for the Old World, but also because the earliest artifacts found are recognized at once as technologically advanced. They must be compared with Neolithic or late Paleolithic phases of culture development of the Old World. And because in the Old World we find the simpler technological conditions which account for the appearance of more advanced work in stone, we accept the Old World as the place of origin and development of the earliest tool technologies found in the Americas.

This basic view of continuity and change, and of growth and development, was one of the fundamental ideas which Tylor, Morgan, Spencer, and other evolutionary anthropologists sought to stress in relation to culture and civilization in the same way that their biological contemporaries developed it in relation to the organic world. They attempted to establish the historical fact that civilizations have a history reaching back into a remote past, that the history of all cultures and of all mankind was interwoven, and that advanced civilizations were developments from more primitive cultures. No doubt they erred in their interpretations of the process undergone; no doubt they were overeager to accept specific historical sequences of cultural events as universal and inevitable serial orders. But the errors of the evolutionists should not blind us to the fact that they set the principle of the historical continuity of culture upon firm foundations, and established the necessity of thinking in terms of historical or sequential change and development.

The principles which we accept in common with them, and which we use so constantly in our work, essentially involve an implicit or explicit recognition of sequence. Events happen in time, and one condition may be superseded by another which is markedly different. The increase of our historical knowledge and understanding about culture has made us increasingly aware of many types of sequential events which have happened in the history of culture. We have come to realize that most cultural conditions cannot be understood as direct expressions of human behavior and activity on the basis of human potentialities at the proto-human level, but must rather be considered advanced or sophisticated cultural developments which necessarily imply special types of earlier cultural conditions as their forerunners. In the most general form, if we had to put into words the types of conditions we have in mind, we would not depart greatly from some at least of the sequential ideas of evolutionists like Morgan, or Hobhouse, or Durkheim, among others.

There is a broad contrast between social and cultural conditions among the simplest peoples and in modern European civilizations which serves as a point of departure. In the case of the former, we find sparse populations living in numerically small groups, composed basically of kinfolk, essentially self-sufficient economically, with no division of labor save in terms of differences of sex and age, without sovereignty or centralized authority, and with a high degree of social and cultural homogeneity within the group. Technologically, we find dependence upon simple, rather than composite tools and materials; economically, a utilization of natural resources mainly as found without important transformation, and with the almost entire absence of importation of materials not found in the local environment; politically a dependence upon non-centralized types of leadership in undertakings; socially a dependence upon unspecialized status and role relationships defined by kinship; and culturally a dependence upon norms which are largely cultural universals, and upon individuals who are essentially microcosms of their culture.

In the case of European civilizations, we find dense populations living in groups which include cities of great size, composed basically of people who are for the most part unrelated by kinship, economically never self-sufficient but interdependent, with intensive division of labor in society and in manufacture, with sovereignty and centralized authority, and with a high degree of social and cultural heterogeneity within the group. Technologically, there is predominantly dependence upon composite and highly specialized tools and processed materials; economically, upon trade and commerce; politically, upon formally organized government; socially upon status and role relationships which are specialized and differentiated in function, with kinship in a functionally attenuated condition; and culturally, to a marked degree upon types of norms which are largely cultural specialties, and upon individuals whose careers of experience may be highly particular and essentially unique.

The simplest societies and European civilization form two extreme contrasts in such respects as these. Other societies show intermediate conditions in many of these respects. We cannot claim, of course, that the particular cultural institutions of any one of the extremely primitive contemporary peoples are exactly like what the original conditions of European civilization were. But there are certain fundamental conditions of concomitant variations which we observe in the contrast between the simplest peoples and modern civilization. In European civilization, the basic institutional forms are complex and differentiated, and clearly call for explanation in terms of historical growth and development. In the case of the simplest societies we have conditions much closer in structure to the proto-human level of culture, in the sense, primarily, that such primitive peoples lack most of the intermediating agencies which our civilization possesses, and are necessarily dependent to a greater degree upon human and natural resources alone. Under such conditions, and in the absence of structural factors such as complex technology, division of labor, control of food supply, and so forth, we find that concomitantly there are also absent such institutional conditions as are roughly summarized as social and cultural heterogeneity, institutional specialization, or formal political and legal organization. This leads to the hypothesis that there may be a causal connection between the advanced structural forms of our own civilization and their modern functional concomitants. And since the historical development of many of these advanced forms can be worked out, we postulate as a working hypothesis that earlier in the history of our civilization, when they were absent, their concomitants were also absent, and conditions, broadly speaking, must have resembled the generalized type of situation known to us from the consideration of the simplest societies taken together.

Actually, we are constantly working with sequential ideas, implicitly if not explicitly, particularly in relation to the sequential order of limited phases of culture. In such cases we have come to recognize implicitly that the presence of certain conditions necessarily implies the earlier presence of certain other preconditions in the history of that cultural development. Many sequential relations of this type are widely accepted. In technology, for example, the use of processed materials, like hard, polished stone, or wood pulp, or alloys, must be later than the use of raw materials as found in their natural state. The use of composite tools, like the Eskimo harpoon, which combine principles or materials into a single functional unit, must succeed in time the use of simple tool units made of single substances. Specialization of tool forms to particular functional uses, involving varieties of axes or hammers in the same technology, must be later than the use of unspecialized tools which serve many functions, like the coup de poing.

The control of food supply by means of preservation and storage is necessarily later than hunting and food gathering conditions in which the food quest is an inevitable daily enterprise. The use of techniques of domestication of animals and plants is historically after an earlier condition of hunting and food gathering. Domestication of animals itself implies a prior condition in which animal forms are used in their wild state; cultivation of plants a prior condition in which wild plant foods are used as found. Intensive methods of cultivation imply an earlier condition of cultivation by more extensive methods. Wherever we have established some condition as a late development, by historical or ancillary evidence, we use the fact in visualizing an earlier implied condition. Thus, since we know the use of metals is later than the use of non-metallic materials, we recognize that a metal-using culture implies earlier conditions in which stone, wood, horn, etc., were the basic materials. Ceramic conditions imply a pre-ceramic past, and every archaeologist uses this chronological fact in his work. Since wild animals do not yield milk, we view dairying cultures as implying a non-dairying earlier form of domestication. Wild sheep cannot be sheared, since they lack woolly hair, hence we recognize that where domesticated use of sheep wool is the condition, it necessarily implies an earlier form of sheep domestication for other functional purposes.

Similar types of sequential views of economic and social forms are widely held, although perhaps we cannot state as detailed and definite sequential postulates because we become involved with aspects of culture of the nature of emergents. These may not be directly connected with one another sequentially, but indirectly through the sequential relations of their structural bases. However, illustrations of commonly accepted sequential relations are not wanting. A division of labor in society implies an earlier condition in which the only distinction of activities is by sex and age. A division of labor in manufacture implies a prior condition of division of labor in society. Specialization in which the individual or group concentrates upon one economic activity and exchanges such goods or services for other consumer goods implies an earlier condition of specialization, like that of arrow makers, artists, or tipi pattern cutters of the Plains, in which individual specialists are jacks or jills of all other techniques at the same time, and do not support themselves by their specialized occupation alone. Trade in essentials, with the community dependent upon it, implies an earlier condition of relatively self-sufficient group life in which needs are met by the activities of members of the group alone. The existence of markets implies a prior condition of trade without markets, and also of specialization and social division of labor. Trade for profit is later than trade for use. Credit systems imply prior conditions of extensive exchange. Money economies imply earlier conditions of barter without a standard medium of exchange. Slavery, as a basic economic mechanism, is necessarily later than conditions in which all members of the group had equal free status. Wage-earning, or employment for hire, implies earlier conditions in which each individual works for himself, and there are no status differences of employer–employee. Caste stratification implies earlier social forms in which there are no hereditary group distinctions. Economic class differences, connected with role in production, imply the coexistence of a division of labor, and hence must be later than classless conditions in the social group. Restricted private ownership of land implies an earlier condition in which land is common or free domain. Conditions in which social relations are predominantly based on status in terms of economic, political, and social non-kinship factors, implies an earlier condition in which status was determined by kinship primarily.

Political organizations like the state imply earlier dependence on clan or kinship group mechanisms of group action. Organized warfare, linked as it is to political organization of the group, implies earlier forms of feud action in terms of kinship and collective responsibility. Composition, linked to the existence of developed property values, is later than feud conditions without mechanisms for property settlement. Warfare for conquest of land is later than fighting to settle wrongs. Formalized legal organization is later than customary legal procedure without established legal organization. Individualization, where wholly unique careers are open to the individual, is linked to cultural heterogeneity, and is necessarily later than conditions of homogeneity in which every individual participates in the whole culture. In more intangible phases of culture, science and rationalism imply earlier conditions of magical procedures and animistic thought; exact logical distinctions of cause and effect are later than anthropomorphic interpretations; the distinction of natural from supernatural is later than an amorphous fusing of the two. In the organization and management of religious, economic, social, and political agencies, specialization and differentiation of function is clearly later than control by unspecialized agencies.

We have also become increasingly aware of links between sequential relations. The development of food preservation and storage, and the invention of techniques of animal and plant domestication, must precede the existence of dense populations and large local groups, and population density in turn is a precondition for increasing social and economic differentiation and interdependence, cultural heterogeneity, and the attenuation of the kinship tie. Cultural heterogeneity has still further effects in the increasing individualization of members of the community.

Most of the illustrations of sequential relations, which I have offered somewhat at random, are not novel. For example, the early kinship basis of society was stressed by Morgan, Hobhouse, Durkheim, Maine, and others. Transition from social and cultural homogeneity to heterogeneity, from absence of division of labor to intensive division of labor, from sparse populations to dense populations, with concomitant effects, has been discussed by many writers. What is more important than the question of novelty is the fact that we do accept the historical fact of sequential relations and make use of them constantly in our work. The questions that remain are what function they can serve in research if made explicit, and how we must limit their meaning.

In the illustrations offered I have attempted to indicate sequences of cultural conditions in time, which are historically true, and in which one state of culture implies the other as a necessary precondition. This is not invalidated by questions of borrowing or diffusion, because we are here referring to relations of the cultural conditions themselves, regardless of the carriers of culture. When we say that a dairying culture implies a precondition of domestication without dairying, this does not mean that the ancestors of some dairying people like the Todas practiced some non-dairying form of domestication. It does assert that the technique of dairying was necessarily preceded technologically by other techniques of domestication, regardless of who the people were who were involved in the development of the technology.

The decided limitation of most of the sequential relations we can historically accept is a scientific and logical one. They are of such a character that the precondition is necessary to the subsequent condition but is not a sufficient causal explanation of what followed. If we assert that a division of labor in society was preceded by sex and age distinctions of activities alone, we cannot claim that we understand how division of labor arose on the basis of that sequence of conditions by itself. Many other factors besides the existence of sex and age distinctions of activities are also necessary causes or preconditions of the appearance of division of labor. These may include special aptitudes, technological developments, trade, increasing population, and accidental historical factors of environment, contact, and borrowing. What we have asserted in the sequential relation is merely the statement of a precondition which is necessarily implied by a subsequent condition. The subsequent condition cannot occur without the preceding condition having happened. But the subsequent condition does not happen merely as a result of the factors in the precondition stated. For such a complete explanation of the development of any cultural form or institution we need a statement not of one necessary precondition, or even of several, but of *all* the necessary and sufficient preconditions which taken together account causally and historically for the appearance of the later phenomenon. The errors of many of the evolutionary theorists clearly involved a failure to make this important distinction. They sought too frequently to interpret a clear-cut and often necessary precondition as a statement of necessary and sufficient conditions, and hence overlooked all of the complex historical factors involved in any cultural development.

The historical nature of the subject matter with which we deal makes the problem of constructing sequences in which we can be sure we have all the necessary and sufficient causal conditions of a later event a difficult undertaking, and it may be that we shall never have that kind of certainty. But the difficulty involved should not blind us to the actual existence of sequences of precondition and subsequent condition, however limited the character of the determining relation of one to the other, on the basis of present knowledge. Such sequential relations, if made explicit, may serve a very real function in our research. This may be clearer if we consider the difference between the type of sequential relations discussed herein and two other types of relation in culture. The archaeologist (and the historical anthropologist) limits himself primarily to relations of sequence which are essentially chronological. The functional social anthropologist is more directly concerned with interrelations within a culture of the general type called adhesions, in which the two terms of the relation stand for contemporaneous events: as, for example, we speak of matrilocal residence occurring *with* matrilineal descent, or vice versa. The sequential relations to which I have referred are chronological, although not immediately successive, and are functional or causal as well, in the sense that one, the later, necessarily implies the other, the earlier. But in this type of sequential relation the later condition supersedes the earlier. The consideration of such conditions is basic to the problem of social or cultural process of change. In stating explicitly such sequences as we can establish to be historically true, we define for ourselves key problems of process. We cannot assert from such explicit sequences, as for example that involving the division of labor, that we understand the whole process of its development, but we can claim from explicit statement of sequence that we have identified a genuine problem of cultural process. How, from an earlier condition in which sex and age distinctions of activity alone existed, did the division of labor develop? What factors in addition to the earlier economic form were involved in its appearance? Similarly, if we recognize the striking contrast between the contemporary non-kinship base and the earlier kinship base of status, we state a genuine problem of cultural development explicitly. What factors have transformed the earlier kinship condition into the modern type of economic and social status differentiation?

Recognition of these types of problems of cultural development has perhaps been too long delayed. Not the least factor in this lack of attention to such problems has been the avoidance of explicit formulations of sequences, and this taboo is in good part the result of over-dogmatic tendencies of the anti-evolutionists of a generation ago. Their criticism of the evolutionists tended to end in a complete nihilism as regards problems of cultural sequence and development. The result has been an undue timidity, even a taboo, as regards such problems.

Their explicit recognition is not subject to the objections taken to the theories of the classical evolutionists and does not conflict with methods and principles now in use, but should rather make additional types of problems clear-cut and deepen the meaning of both historical and functional research.

6   Social fields and the evolution of society

Amid a good deal of tumult and shouting, social and cultural evolution have taken their place in anthropology alongside biological evolution as facts of human history. There is no longer dispute that "present civilizations are historically continuous with past culture, as far back as we have evidence," that complex culture and society evolved from simpler conditions through a "process of growth, accretion, specialization, and differentiation" (Lesser 1952:139 [Chapter 5]). Present debate concerns *how* the evolutionary process took place – in general, and in relation to particular sequences of change; and seeks concepts and theory that systematize or unify the vast panorama of historical time – space events which are the matrix of social evolution.

It has not been so for long. In 1939, when I discussed "Evolution in Social Anthropology" (Lesser 1952 [Chapter 5]) at Association meetings in Chicago, I had been warned by a social scientist who was by no means extreme in his view that "evolution" was a dirty, dangerous word, and urged to replace it by the word "development." I took the position at that time that the subject matter in which evolutionary change or sequence must be studied is historical in character, and I continue to believe in this directive and this limitation. Whatever the value of a philosophy of social or cultural evolution, I think that the anthropologist, as scientist, must be true to his subject matter, its historical dimensions, and its factual limitations.

From this standpoint I want to call to mind an obvious reality of human social and cultural history that has been given too little weight in discussions of social evolution – the phenomena long recognized in such concepts as borrowing and diffusion.

As facts of history, of course, borrowing and diffusion are beyond dispute. Here I will refer only to the general evidence that they are features

This article was originally published in *Southwestern Journal of Anthropology* 17 (1961):40–8. Reproduced by permission of the *Journal of Anthropological Research* (formerly *SWJA*).

of human history from the beginning. Thus, in the Paleolithic, there is the distinction between the hand-ax cultural tradition and the flake tradition; each of which is of great, possibly equal, antiquity; each of which is found in many sites over a wide continental range (Oakley 1959). Archaeologists agree that the distribution of each tradition implies contact and influence among many of the peoples and settlements who shared it. How else can we account for hand-axes from sites at great distances from one another so identical in form and size that often they can be distinguished only by the materials used?

Although borrowing and diffusion are evident from early times and must probably be assumed normal throughout human history, they have been taken into account for the most part only in so-called "historical" or "historical reconstruction" studies; or used primarily, in early work, as a ready (and perhaps superficial) explanation of social and cultural similarities between neighboring peoples. Little attention was given the phenomena of borrowing or diffusion in the analysis of society. That analysis was focused upon a particular social aggregate, conceived as a distinct and separate society, and the impact of other aggregates upon the one under consideration was usually treated as external, essentially fortuitous or accidental. The study of social process, social change, or social evolution became largely an analysis of phenomena found *within* a social aggregate, delimited as a social isolate. For purposes of analysis, the external social environment was stripped away; it was a realm of historical accident which obscured the system of relations that constituted the essential process of the inner life of *a* society.

But such concepts as diffusion and borrowing, and the contact to which they refer, have a fundamental implication which cannot be ignored: that any one social aggregate – group, settlement, community, tribe – is involved with others, that an interdependent influence of social aggregates upon one another is virtually universal. And there is a further implication – that this interdependent involvement of social aggregates cannot be a matter of haphazard, chance contacts. It may be possible to conceive that certain cultural items, like a story or a type of implement, may be diffused or borrowed in the course of incidental or chance contact, though even this seems historically unlikely. But it is impossible to conceive that diffusions (implied by distributions) of forms of marriage and descent, clan structure, political institutions, or systematized religious beliefs, have taken place in such a manner. Much more fundamental interpersonal relations between people of different social aggregates are required to explain such phenomena. It may be necessary to conceive human social life and human history as a time and space continuum of human association.

If that be the reality, how can it be disregarded as extraneous and adventitious in analysis of social process, social change, and social evolution? How can a single delimited social aggregate, isolated from its matrix of human associations, be treated as society or human society, and the processes of human social life be studied exclusively within it?

Yet the myth of the primitive isolate is still with us, still embedded in current concept and theory. Robert Redfield, for example, a leading spokesman for the concept of the primitive isolate, recognized in his *Peasant Society and Culture* that the conception is inapplicable to peasantry, as "part-societies," but still clung to it as the essential abstraction of primitive society and as a conceptual model which may have continuing, if more limited, usefulness in research on more complex society (Redfield 1956, chaps. 1–2; see also 1947; 1953; 1955).

Adherents of the theory of the primitive isolate, of course, recognize that it may be impossible to find and difficult to conceive *a* society that is physically or socially isolated in an absolute sense at any level from primitive to modern. Yet they imply that isolation, as the extreme opposite of the contact so obvious in complex social situations, be imagined to have been the condition at the beginning; and draw from this hypothetical notion that idea of the primitive isolate as a conceptual tool. One is reminded of how some nineteenth-century evolutionists postulated promiscuity – the absence of patterned interpersonal sexual relations – as the primitive social condition from which marriage and the family had evolved.

The conception of the primitive isolate compels one to view early or primitive human life as a world of closed social aggregates, each out of contact with other humans.[11] It involves what Gideon Sjoberg (1959:352–3) has referred to as a preoccupation with "closed systems," of which both anthropologists and sociologists have been guilty; and it would appear that much of the discussion of "holism" as *the* anthropological approach entails this preoccupation. The early functionalists who made a fetish of exclusively synchronic study left diachronic phenomena, history, out. History in their view might be interesting in a descriptive sense; but, with its concern for borrowing and diffusion, it was about "origins" and irrelevant to the analysis of social process within a closed social system.

I propose to ask what difference it makes if we adopt as a working hypothesis the universality of human contact and influence – as a fundamental feature of the socio-historical process; if we conceive of human societies – prehistoric, primitive, or modern – not as closed systems, but as open systems; if we think of any social aggregate not as isolated, separated by some kind of wall, from others, but as inextricably involved with other aggregates, near and far, in weblike, netlike connections.

The concept of social field, or field of social relations, being developed and used by British social anthropologists – Fortes (1949); Gluckman (1949); Firth (1951); Barnes (1954), among others – seems to fit the realities of socio-historical human situations, so described. Firth has put it concisely: "Fields of social relations, not clear-cut societies, must be the more empirical notion of social aggregates" (Firth 1951:28). In this discussion I suggest the concept be understood in the sense of Durkheim's statement of many years ago: "There is no people and no state which is not part of another society, more or less unlimited, which embraces all the peoples and all the states with which the first comes in contact, either directly or indirectly" (Durkheim 1915:426, cited in Honigmann 1959:17).[12]

The concept of social field has a fundamental implication: social relations within the field are patterned, not unstructured, adventitious, or incidental. The concept of patterns of culture is now a byword. But it has been used almost exclusively to describe interpersonal relations between members of the same social aggregate. Yet the evidence strongly indicates that interpersonal relations between members of different social aggregates – groups, tribes, communities, settlements – are similarly patterned. One calls to mind Malinowski's famous kula ring of the Trobriands. Yet that is not an exceptional phenomenon. Where trade relations among primitives are explicitly described – American Indian, Australian, Melanesian, African – trade partnerships and/or structured friendships – traditional patterning of interpersonal relations – are similarly in evidence. Intermarriage, visiting and travel, feud and rights of asylum, war and peace-making and attendant capture and/or adoption involve in the same way patterned intergroup relations that can be described in terms of norms and traditional behavior. G. C. Wheeler pointed this out long ago in his *The Tribe and Intertribal Relations in Australia* (1910).

Much of the phenomena of borrowing and diffusion, as already noted, imply structured interpersonal relations. For example, Goldman showed some years ago how the incongruous diffusion of potlatching and inherited crest prerogatives from the affluent Northwest Coast to the interior Alkatcho Carrier of British Columbia, with their relatively impoverished economy, could be understood in terms of trade and marriage between the Carrier and the Bella Coola. Long established trade relations, intensified by the coming of the fur trade, stimulated intermarriage between coast and interior families to consolidate and maintain trade connections. Marriage brought with it, as an integral part of its pattern, potlatch feasting and inherited prerogatives (see Goldman 1941). Again, in the Southwest, the diffusion of clan forms from Pueblo peoples to Athapascan Navahos and Apaches involved long continued association – including trade relations between particular Pueblos and particular Athapascan groups during the early period of Athapascan penetration of the region – and residence and marriage, at various times, of Pueblo people among Navahos and Apaches.

Thus, within a field of social relations interpersonal relations are structured and patterned. Conversely, when structured or patterned relations are found – or are implied by other evidence – a field of social relations is involved, embracing more than one social aggregate and usually a considerable number.

The social field concept, so understood, can I believe help to resolve important problems of social evolution. In this brief discussion I propose only to offer some illustrative suggestions – in particular, on the appearance of surplus and the origins of the division of labor.

The traditional view of surplus in discussions of social evolution, followed by Childe and others, is essentially that it is an unanticipated emergent of technological development – the domestication of plants, initially. Technology is in this view an independent variable, its development or evolution left unexplained. Technological changes lead to increased food production, in quantities greater than those needed by the producer, resulting in surplus. Surplus in turn is then a precondition of and a factor in the appearance of craft specialization. Some members of the group produce food for all; some are released for other work. Under some form of leadership or group authority, a division of work may then even be assigned (see Childe 1936, 1946, 1951).

This view betrays the preoccupation with social aggregates as closed systems referred to above. If social aggregates are viewed as open systems in a field of social relations, it seems clear that Neolithic cultivation of plants developed in a region in which widespread intergroup relations were going on, including economic relations of exchange as well as social relations. There is I believe adequate evidence, summarized by Childe himself, for Neolithic and even pre-Neolithic trade. In addition, I think it can be stated as a general hypothesis that in *any* region in which social aggregates differ in what they produce, exchange between aggregates is probable. In the Neolithic, in maintaining or extending social and economic relations, those at either end of the exchange found it advantageous to produce what they habitually exchanged or could exchange in sufficient quantities to meet their exchange obligations as well as their own needs. Demand then, in the sense of obligations and requirements involved in on-going exchange relationships, was related to supply. *We* refer to what was produced for exchange, and not for immediate domestic needs, as *surplus*.

This conception clarifies the meaning and appearance of surplus and at the same time indicates the motivations probably involved. It is suggestive too on the problem of technological improvement and invention, and why it may happen, making such change an interdependent rather than an independent variable. Production *may* be increased to meet obligation demands without change of technology – by planting more fields in the same manner, for example. *Or*, it may be increased by inventing or discovering new, more productive techniques. The appearance of hybridization during the Neolithic, for example, obviously implies intention and purpose. It can hardly have been an accidental discovery or some inevitable technological evolution independent of the social situation in which it occurred and the human motivations active therein.

Thus, from the social field approach, technological change and improvement as well as the appearance and meaning of surplus are functional aspects of a field of social and economic relations.

The appearance of division of labor can be similarly understood. Differences in the products exchanged between members of different social aggregates may result in group specialization. Members of one group become more dependent on members of another for certain products secured by exchange, and as a result may become regional specialists in the production of the goods required for exchange. In the American Indian Plains, for example, during the pedestrian period, Apaches and Kiowas traded meat and skin products with Arikara villagers for tobacco and corn (Hyde 1959). Although within each Plains group activities were differentiated only by sex and age – each man a hunter, each woman a skin worker – the men smoked tobacco and men and women ate corn which they did not produce, which they obtained by trade. Group specialization and a regional division of labor were taking place within a field of economic relations.

Childe (1951) refers to this type of situation, in discussing prehistory, as *inter*communal specialization, and distinguishes it from *intra*communal specialization (see index in Childe 1951 for page references to specialization). The data he provides suggest that the former – intercommunal specialization – may precede the latter – intracommunal specialization – in time and in evolution. But *intra*communal specialization, division of labor within one social aggregate, seems primarily a more intensive development of group specialization in relation to regional exchange, and its appearance *can* be contemporary with intercommunal specialization, rather than later. Thus, when members of a single social aggregate produce more than one product which is involved in regional exchange and group specialization, specialization may arise within the group as different individuals concentrate on different products to meet their exchange obligations. This may be seen in as primitive a society as the Bushman of South Africa. Bands that are linked in a chain of trade for iron and tobacco show tendencies toward both group specialization and individual specialization. The latter occurs where individuals may completely specialize as arrow-makers or even honey-gatherers and trade not only outside their own bands but within them for other products they need (Schapera 1930:145–7).

Conceiving the origins of division of labor in this way as a functional aspect of a field of economic exchange relations avoids the artificial over-rationalization of the traditional view. The idea that division of labor follows from surplus seems to call for a deux ex machina – some central agency which in effect plans and institutes a division of labor and assigns work activities. A field theory makes the interpolation of such extraneous factors unnecessary. At the same time it overcomes difficulties inherent in the view that the beginnings of division of labor can be found in the social and economic structure of particular social aggregates by studies of part-time specialization – like that of the tipi pattern-cutter or the tipi-painter of the American Indian Plains. Full-time specialization is not accounted for in such limited studies; the factors and functional relations included are not adequate by themselves to explain it. The theory proposed, by contrast, provides an adequate basis of explanation by enlarging the analysis to take into account factors of exchange or trade, of economic and social relations within a larger field.

The hypothesis that division of labor arises as a function of a field of economic relations and exchange offers a general theory that can be analyzed and tested in many historical situations. For example, it supports the thesis that pastoral cultures, even in early times, were probably specializations or part-cultures in the economic sense, linked in a symbiotic relation to agricultural peoples in a social and economic field (Kroeber 1948:276–7, 690–1). Or, in the modern period, it seems clear that the industrial revolution in England, essentially a further intensification of division of labor, arose while England was part of a far-flung web or network of mercantile trade relations. The rapid growth of the triangular trade with coastal Africa for slaves and with the West Indies for plantation products was a major factor in stimulating production of manufactured goods at home; first by causing an increase in domestic handicraft production, later by stimulating the invention of new techniques for further increasing production. Trade demands made for increased production and then improved methods of production.

The social field concept as the basic social reality, rather than distinct societies or social aggregates, may clarify other evolutionary problems, for example, the evolution of political and legal institutions. It suggests that centralized political or legal authority develops within a field of political and legal relations, and not in isolated, closed social units considered separately. The conquest theory of the state, stripped of its particularities, essentially means that the *relations* of social aggregates within a field are the primary factors in the development of state forms and class-structured states.

The suggestion offered, then, is that the field concept rather than the concept of society as an isolate or closed system reflects socio-historical realities more accurately – that human contact and patterned interpersonal relations are not restricted to social interaction within a single localized social aggregate, but are a universal constant of social life. From this standpoint, there is a communications process between any social aggregate, primitive or more advanced, and others. The communications process has evolved, but it has not evolved out of conditions in which it was absent, but from the primitive communications process which links social aggregates even in the earliest time of which we have evidence.[13]

The field concept, I suggest, is particularly useful in understanding social evolutionary change that has taken place in human history. It unites into one field the study of those patterned interpersonal relations usually considered external, or merely a matter of historical accident, and those that are an integral part of a particular social aggregate. It breaks down the notion that history involves mere happenstance which interferes with analysis of social process in systems of relations, of order and regularity in events. History and synchronic analysis become parts of one universe of discourse, of one order or level of the human social process.

Part IV

Anthropology and modern life

Introduction to Part IV

The four works in this fourth and final section were written at different periods in Lesser's professional life. They cohere because all are related to his lifelong desire to make anthropology an instrument of practical, policy-relevant understanding. The first three essays deal with the American Indians; the fourth, Lesser's last significant scholarly piece, previously unpublished, deals with the world order. In each the concern is with issues at once immediate and serious, issues on which many anthropologists believe the discipline has something useful to contribute. Some of us would go further – I believe Lesser would – and say that it is either disingenuous or falsely modest to opt for a supposedly value-free social science without also granting that anthropology is at least potentially useful in the solution of social problems.

Lesser's publications on Indians and policy are numerous; among them, "The right not to assimilate" (Chapter 7) is outstanding. It raises in clear fashion two facts about North America and North American Indians that are only rarely acknowledged in public. The first is that many North American Indians do not want, and never have wanted, to be "just like the rest of us." The second is that though North American Indians feel this way, and though there is absolutely no reason why they should feel differently, this feeling is a source of great discomfort to other North Americans, a discomfort with which we as a people are reluctant to deal. By calling attention to this situation, Lesser is chronicling the North American myth. The citizens of most large nations understand that there are many other people who don't want to be "just like them," even if these citizens consider themselves superior to the nonconformists. "Mainstream Americans," however, have trouble accepting that idea. They are also troubled by cultures (both inside the United States and outside it) that are not responsive to opportunities to forgo some intangible benefits for the privilege of heightened consumption, and they are likely to view such behavior as a criticism of themselves. Most of our families have been converted into "Americans" very recently. Most of us have accepted the conversion with open arms, and to discover that Indians may believe otherwise is apparently quite disturbing. Indeed, that this really is their land makes their unwillingness to buy our message even more maddening to some of us. Lesser's imaginative handling of this issue and its political implications is, again, a substantial step beyond Boas.

The essay entitled "The cultural significance of the Ghost Dance" (Chapter 8) was presented orally in 1931, two years after Lesser was awarded his doctorate, and published in 1933, the same year his monograph, *The Pawnee Ghost Dance Hand Game*, first appeared. The paper was a kind of preface to the monograph, stressing the social utility of the Ghost Dance as an opportunity for cultural reintegration, for both preservation and invention:

In short, the activity of the Ghost Dance times was not a mere revival of old ways, it became a renaissance of Pawnee culture.

This effect occurred in the following way: In a vision the subject would "see" some old way of life which had come to be disregarded. He would "remember" it. His vision then became a command upon those alive who knew how it must be carried out, to do so. Sometimes there were men alive who knew the thing thoroughly and were persuaded by the demand of such a supernatural message to begin it again. But often a ritual or dance was only partially remembered. Then many men would get together and pool their memories to review the affair. If the "seen" phase of old life was social and non-esoteric, the visionary himself would revive the old way. Hence games, and hand games (Lesser 1933 [Chapter 8]).

Lesser goes on to explain how performances that once would have been sacrilegious to the Pawnee became required under the influence of the Ghost Dance religion, imposing an internal revivification of Pawnee culture. He saw that this phenomenon was also in important ways a reclaiming of the past as a human right, with all the elements of group resistance and rediscovery such events embody. He builds brilliantly on the early observations of the great ethnographer James Mooney, who treated the Ghost Dance as a form of protest (see Mooney 1896). Lesser was one of the few scholars who early recognized the importance of Mooney's analysis as a document of cultural recovery, or restoration.

Though it may not be apparent in a superficial reading, Lesser's reconstruction of the significance of the Ghost Dance as a socioreligious process also illuminates the early history of Afro-American cultures. In both, anthropologists are compelled to deal with profoundly disturbed social systems, within which people seek in some organized manner to refashion new cultural forms out of older materials (see, for instance, Mintz and Price 1976). An implicit assumption in much of the work on social and cultural change was that subject peoples would improve themselves by assimilating the cultures of their conquerors. Both American Indians and Black Americans were expected to do so, and thus to "civilize" themselves. Resistance has therefore often meant a search for ancestral traditions that might be rewoven into some coherent form through which people could identify themselves collectively, in cultural and ideological contradistinction to those more powerful than they. Lesser's early paper and his monograph on the hand game are important theoretical building-blocks in that perspective.

The foreword to the 1978 edition of *The Pawnee Ghost Dance Hand Game* (Chapter 9) was written toward the end of Lesser's scholarly life. It graces one of the genuinely important monographs written by Boas's "second generation" of students, one unjustly (and almost mysteriously) ignored by the discipline until the University of Wisconsin Press decided to produce a paperback edition of it in 1978. Lesser says relatively little about the hand game in this new foreword, but he does provide us with a view of the circumstances under which the monograph was written. This piece also contains what was probably Lesser's last written espousal of a historical perspective in anthropology.

The reissue of the monograph so many years after its original publication was a tribute not only to its enduring quality but also to the freshness and vitality of its ideas. Yet few people other than anthropological specialists on the Plains Indians have read this remarkable work thoroughly. It is ethnological and historical, minutely detailed, particularistic, and intensely focused. The dramatization of the plight of American Indians in recent decades, though understandable, has distracted us from the importance of the everyday in the life of these peoples. Because Lesser's analysis, in its narrowest focus, is about a game – a game associated with a dance – it is not the sort of thing the casual reader is likely to study carefully, let alone associate with the massacre at Wounded Knee, with Custer's Last Stand, or with Geronimo or Chief Joseph.

Detailed and demanding of the reader, the monograph's strengths are many, not the least that it was far ahead of its time, both in its formulation of a theory of culture and in the application of that theory.

Lesser does not start with the Ghost Dance or the Hand Game. Instead, he starts with the Pawnee and the whole absymal record of their subjugation to the United States government and its caprices. Herein is one of the best and most unvarnished records of U.S.-Indian relations ever to be written by an anthropologist – indeed, an account quite unmatched when it first appeared. Lesser then turns to the Ghost Dance, that remarkable effusion of feeling and identity, when the past and the future were fused together in act and enactment by the immense power of shared feeling. Whereas the shorter essay (Chapter 8) treats the Ghost Dance more in terms of its general meaning for a theory of social and cultural change (thus anticipating much later work, e.g., Wallace 1965, La Barre 1970), the monograph describes the Ghost Dance in rich detail and sets it deep within Pawnee culture, preparing us to examine the hand game.

Even though its presentation is both detailed and intricate, Lesser's argument is fundamentally quite simple: He takes the position that what the game *means* – why people play it, with what purpose or to what ends it is played, who plays it, and under what circumstances – can only be understood in the historical context of its changing character. Not only did hand games change in form over time, how they fit within the culture also changed. Lesser writes of "the renaissance of culture which took place among the Pawnee under the stimulus of the Ghost Dance," then concentrates on the hand games associated with the Ghost Dance: "The controlled consideration of the games in their changing forms has made it possible to consider the meaning of processes of change, and the inevitability of founding ethnological methodology on a metaphysic of history" (Lesser 1978:xxv–xxvi).

These words from the introduction to *The Pawnee Ghost Dance Hand Game* were written in 1932, when Lesser was still a young man, and at the threshold of his professional career. Yet they epitomize the contribution to anthropology he would make in the course of subsequent decades. If there is one feature above all others that has distinguished Lesser's contribution to anthropology, it is his stress upon history. In contrast to the British functionalists, Boas's contemporaries, for whom whatever had a contemporary existence must also have had a contemporary meaning/function/use – for whom, that is, there was no such thing as a survival – Lesser always saw history as written upon the behavior of groups in their institutional forms: "In human culture, as in human experience, what has come to attention and prominence never disappears. Either it is retained in some form as part of culture thereafter, or it leaves its impress and influence upon other aspects of culture" (Lesser 1933 [Chapter 8]).

His insistence on the importance of history and the historical method never blinded him to the intricate interrelationship among features of culture at any one point in time. Indeed, when he writes of history and historicity, it is *always* with a stress upon the interrelatedness of phenomena: "We know nothing of things save insofar as we can define and control their interrelations or interconnections with other things, and it is an inevitable part of such investigation to note the different modes and intensities of these functional interrelations." For Lesser, "history" is not explanation, and it is "neither an end nor by itself a means but a condition that must be recognized at every step" (Lesser 1978:335–6).

By constantly infusing his historical description with a consideration of the relations among different institutions, and by giving his functional treatment a historical perspective, Lesser not only exemplified the best that anthropology has to offer the student of society, but led the way toward its methodological improvement.

The final paper in this volume expresses many of the themes that concerned Lesser in his scholarly work: the cultural variability and changeability of the human species; the social (as opposed to biological or innate) basis for group behavior; the rights of human groups to defend and perpetuate their respective cultural forms; the need for societal planning in the solution of conflict. In writing this essay, Lesser returned repeatedly to the lessons he had learned from his teacher, Boas. But he added a distinctive imprint to those ideas, drawing on his own work on social boundaries, the right not to assimilate, social evolution, and the social and political origins of war. The cynical reader may find him too optimistic, or judge him naïve. But Lesser's persuasiveness is to be found in his careful discussion of the persistence of ethnicity, of the limitations of nationalism, of the unscientific basis of racism. In a world that grows smaller each day, Lesser emerges as the realist and, more important, as the scientist. This final essay is in many ways his credo as scientist and as citizen.

7 The right not to assimilate: the case of the American Indian

To a good many Americans, the American Indians are a "problem," and by no means a simple problem that can be easily solved. This rather common American feeling cannot be accounted for alone by the position of the Indians as a minority or by the disadvantages that go with it. In actual situations of discrimination, the public mood is clear and action prompt. Thus, in Pontiac, Michigan, in 1960, when a Winnebago veteran was denied burial in a cemetery "restricted to Caucasians," the people were indignant and interred him with public ceremony and military honors. This kind of Indian "problem" is unlikely to leave vague discomforts unresolved.

The sense that Indians are a special "problem" comes, I think, from their unique position rather than from their minority situation – their distinctive legal status in relation to the nation and their stubborn insistence on their Indian identity. Neither of these is clearly understood by the public, and the intrusion of either or both may so color a situation that public reaction is confused and uncertain. The recent situation in New York illustrates this. Edmund Wilson in *Apologies to the Iroquois* (1960) observed that in Niagara Falls "a good deal of sympathy . . . for the fight of the Tuscaroras" against New York Power Authority plans to take Tuscarora lands for a hydroelectric project "turned into a kind of resentment" when the Indians, invoking tribal rights under treaties with the United States, seemed to be winning; non-Indians in the same predicament have no such legal argument against condemnation. This kind of situation may not evoke a definitive public reaction; it is more likely to generate uneasiness and leave behind it a sense of "problems" unresolved.

This paper originally circulated in 1961 as Occasional Paper No. 3 of the Phelps-Stokes Fund, and was published as "Education and the future of tribalism in the U.S.," in *Social Science Service Review* 35:135–43. © 1961 The University of Chicago Press. Reproduced by permission.

A resolution of this special Indian "problem" is unlikely unless the factors involved in the Indian situation are understood and unless the historical significance of the position of the Indians in the United States is realized.

I

Americans not in direct contact with Indians may not even be aware of their existence most of the time, and the experience of rediscovery, when Indians make headlines, may itself be disturbing. Indians are a reminder of a past that troubles the American conscience. More than that, their existence as *Indians* unsettles the firm conviction that in this country, with its superior institutions, assimilation is proper and desirable and in fact an inevitable, automatic process. Why, after centuries of contact with us, should Indians still feel so separate and aloof?

In 1961, the striking fact is that Indians are not only here with us to stay, in the sense of biological survival,[14] but that there are many thousands of Indians – in 29 of the 50 states – still essentially unassimilated. They have not experienced that identification of interests and outlook, that "interpenetration and fusion," in which they would have acquired American "memories, sentiments, and attitudes" and come to share our "experiences and history" which the late Chicago sociologist Robert E. Park saw as the essence of assimilation.

Most unassimilated Indians live in Indian communities. There are many – in twenty-five states. Pueblo and Hopi communities of New Mexico and Arizona and the Navajos are perhaps best known. In the Southwest are also Apache communities, the Pima and the Papago and the Havasupai, among others. But Indian communities are found as well in other parts of the country. To mention a sample, there are the Eastern Cherokees of North Carolina; the Chippewas of Red Lake, Minnesota; the Menominis of Wisconsin; the Sauk and Fox of Iowa; the Hidatsa, Mandan, Arikara, and several divisions of Teton Sioux in the Dakotas; the Blackfeet and Cheyennes in Montana; the Klamaths in Oregon. Other states in which Indian groups survive include Oklahoma, California, Nebraska, Kansas, Wyoming, Idaho, and Washington. Americans recently became aware of two in New York, the Tuscaroras and the Senecas, when these Iroquois opposed state and federal plans to inundate Iroquois lands by construction of dams for power and flood control. Edmund Wilson, in memorializing these people in *Apologies to the Iroquois*, gives eloquent testimony to the viable group life of these and other Iroquois communities of New York.

In size, these communities range from the Navajos, the largest, with more than 70,000 members, to small communities like the Sauk and Fox of Iowa, who number a few hundred. In culture, there is great diversity, and Indians still tend to identify themselves first as Navajos, Sioux, or Cherokees, and secondarily as Indians.

These Indian groups are of course only a handful of the tribes who originally peopled the country. But their endurance, with the deep sense of tradition and identity which many retain, is a remarkable phenomenon. They have survived the exterminations which depleted and destroyed Indian peoples of the Atlantic seaboard and of California; the forced evacuations which took many from their homes into alien country; and the concentration of tribal groups in restricted areas, stripped of their traditional land base. Most important of all, they have survived despite the generations of national effort to force assimilation upon them, for our dominant Indian policy from the beginning has been assimilation. Their existence today reflects the voluntary decision of their members, as citizens of the United States,[15] to maintain traditional group life, in many cases on the homelands of their ancestors – a decision which speaks strongly for the vitality of the Indian way and the values of Indian group life.

How "Indian" is life in these communities? Measured by externals, by clothes and housing, by use of non-Indian technology and gadgets, or by ways in which many now make a living, it may appear that the people of these communities have on the whole adopted our ways. The San Carlos Apaches of New Mexico, for example, raise some of the finest American livestock for market. The Red Lake Chippewas of Minnesota ship fish by refrigerated trucks for sale in Chicago. The Sauk and Fox of Iowa make a living by working for wages among their non-Indian neighbors. Indian life has not been standing still. The Indians have been making accommodations and adjustments to our society and economy from early times, and they continue to do so.

But modern studies of Indian communities show that adoption of the externals of American life is not neatly correlated with accompanying changes in basic Indian attitudes, mind, and personality. Feelings and attitudes, the life of the inner man, change more slowly than utilitarian features of comfort and convenience. Studies among the Cherokees of North Carolina, for example – considered one of the Five Civilized Tribes for more than a century – and among the Navajos of the Southwest reveal the same inner Indian feelings about the world and man's feelings about the world and man's place in nature, the same non-competitive attitudes, the same disinterest in the American drive for progress and change.

The changes these community Indians have made over time, taken all in all, seem selective. Some inner man resisted complete annihilation of self and identify and held fast to values and attitudes acquired in a mother's arms and on a father's knee and chose from us some things of use but not others. They chose principally what we call material culture and technology and little of our sentiments and values and our philosophy of life.

II

Indian non-assimilation in an America which has so largely assimilated many peoples from many lands is an anachronism only if we think of the Indians as merely one among many American minorities and if we look for the same process of cultural change and adjustment in them all. The others are immigrant minorities; with the exception of the Negroes, they came here voluntarily, and their coming, their choice of a new homeland, implies some commitment toward assimilation.

The Indian situation and Indian relations with the dominant culture in America are quite different. The Indians have roots deeply buried in the soil; their communities have a history in the land more ancient than that of the majority people. They can best be compared with European national minorities who became part of an alien country as a result of national expansion or, in North America, with the French-Canadians of Quebec who became part of an English country after 1763. In these cases, as among the Indian communities, the people are resistant to assimilation and try to maintain traditional ways and even traditional language.

What is true of those who remain at home in close association with their own ethnic community, however, is not true of those who may migrate and take up life elsewhere. Members of European national minorities may move into industrial cities or emigrate to America; French-Canadians of Quebec may migrate to western provinces of Canada; American Indians may leave their tribal communities for life in our towns and cities. As in the case of European immigration to the United States, Canada, or Latin America, the migration is a movement of individuals and families.

If they do not return home, these migrants are subject to assimilating influences of a different culture to a degree that their kinfolk at home are not, and they are more likely to be receptive to assimilation. The process takes time and usually takes place over generations. The original migrants achieve only partial assimilation; their children, especially when schooled entirely in the new environment, carry the process further; and in the third generation assimilation becomes virtually complete.

This kind of assimilation has taken place over the years among our Indians, as individuals or families have left their communities and in time severed their tribal connections. How many have left Indianism behind in this way we do not know, for it is difficult to keep an accurate count, but there have been many.

A confusion between this process of assimilation of migrants over a period of generations and that of the adaptive change and accommodation going on in Indian home communities may explain the confident predictions made on more than one occasion that this or that Indian community would become fully assimilated in some definite period of time. The stated period is often twenty-five years, approximately a generation. At the end of that time, however, contrary to predictions, the community is still there, as strong in numbers and as viable and unassimilated as ever. Some members may have left and chosen assimilation, but an increase of the population at home has usually more than made up for the loss. It has become increasingly probable that many of the communities that have endured are likely to be with us for a long and indefinite future unless radical or brutal measures are taken to disorganize and disperse them. We may have to come to terms with a people who seem determined to have a hand in shaping their own destiny.

Nor is the persistence of these Indian communities in an industrialized America a wholly exceptional fact in the modern world. Communities with strong commitments to traditional way of life are known in industrialized European areas. For example, the Keurs, in *The Deeply Rooted*, describe a traditional Drents community in the Netherlands. More striking are studies in Wales and Cumberland, close to the heart of industrial England, the original home of the Industrial Revolution. Alwyn Rees, in *Life in a Welsh Countryside*, found country neighborhood patterns of life persisting in Wales in 1940 from a pre-industrial past and, in some ways, from a more remote pastoral and tribal past. W. M. Williams, in *Gosforth*, describes Cumberland ways in 1950 still unassimilated by industrial England, still persisting in traditional patterns hundreds of years old.

Such obstinate endurance, with its inner resistance to engulfment by dominant but alien traditions, can be understood, no doubt, as a reflection of the fundamental role of primary relationships – especially that of parents and children – in handing on basic attitudes, feelings, and patterns of interpersonal relations. But it is also a stubborn fact of vital importance in understanding the contemporary world of many peoples and many cultures, each of which may seek from the West ways to improve standards of life, but each of which may at the same time be determined to keep an identity and tradition of its own.

III

The feeling that Indians are a special "problem" is not a reaction only to Indian non-assimilation. The unique legal status of Indians, when it obtrudes and reveals that Indians may have special rights other citizens do not have, is equally disturbing. It offends the American sense of fitness and equality, the feeling that there should be no special groups – none at a disadvantage and none that have advantages over others.

For it is true that the distinctive legal position of the Indians – their primary relation to the federal government – involves what may be called "special rights." The government, as trustee, protects Indian lands, and such trust-protected lands are exempt from state and local taxation.[16] The federal government provides services to Indians, including agricultural and soil conservation services and health and education services, that others receive principally through state and local agencies. And Indian communities have under federal law rights of community self-government and the right to organize tribal business corporations.

The federal status of Indian communities began in early times, and it has a long history. For more than a century after colonization, the balance of power was on the Indian side, and the colonists, seeking peaceful relations essential to the survival and expansion of settlement, dealt with the Indian tribes as they found them – autonomous and self-governing. They made treaties and agreements with individual tribes through tribal leaders.

This recognition of the autonomy of the separate Indian tribes became a principle of dealing with them as independent nations which the United States inherited from British colonial rule. Thus, Indian relations were external affairs of the United States – a matter for treaty-making by the nation and not by the states. We "bought the United States" from the Indians, to use a phrase of Felix Cohen's,[17] by treaties with the individual Indian tribes, treaties which, as part of the bargain, guaranteed trust protection of remaining Indian lands and freedom from taxation on those lands. When the treaty-making period was ended by Congress in 1871, the Indians, as dependent groups within the nation, remained a federal responsibility and the provisions of treaties made before 1871 became continuing federal obligations to the Indians, the basis of most of the "special rights."

The special status of Indians and their "special rights" not only are themselves annoying to us but seem related to that other needling fact about Indians: the aloof pride with which many have persisted in remaining Indian. For their status and rights set the Indians apart, a unique group of American citizens, and thus aid and abet them in keeping a separate identity. On the whole, however, they help those remain Indian who want to be Indian, who express their wish by clinging together in a community; those who want assimilation can and do leave the community and go their separate ways.

During the more than a century of this country's commitment to a policy of assimilating and absorbing the Indians, the government has not been unaware of the role of Indian community life and the federal Indian tie in thwarting the assimilation process. In 1887, Congress saw Indian patterns of land tenure as the foundation of Indian community institutions and attacked them in the General Allotment Act. That act, by ending communal land tenure and making Indians individual property owners, was intended to break up tribal life and assimilate Indians as individuals; unhappily, when communities disintegrated under its pressures, the detribalized individuals who lost their lands became, not assimilated Americans, but paupers and public charges.[18] As recently as 1953, Congress proposed to terminate the federal Indian tie as rapidly as possible, including termination of trust protection and federal services to Indians. The intent was clear: immigrants do not become fully assimilated as tribal groups and neither would Indians. Although the termination program is at a standstill for the present, two large tribes, the Menominis of Wisconsin and the Klamaths of Oregon, are now going through the last stages of termination procedures enacted in 1954.

If it be admitted that the persistence of Indian communities is related to their federal status, and that Indian rejection of full assimilation is related to the fact that Indian communities survive, there still remains the question: Should the nation's Indian policy be committed to and directed toward assimilation?

For a brief period, while John Collier was Commissioner of Indian Affairs (1933–45), this question was courageously answered in the negative. The existence of Indian communities as a reality of the modern world was accepted and a program was designed, partly realized in legislation – the Indian Reorganization Act (IRA) of 1934 and supplementary legislation – to provide Indian communities with the legal status and machinery and the economic resources and opportunities they required to continue their existence for as long a time as they chose. Tribal self-government and tribal business corporations under this program have already been mentioned; the program also included provisions for an adequate land base, financial credit, and adequate training and education.

The charge that this program was intended to halt Indian progress and keep Indians, like museum specimens, in their ancient unchanging ways, stems from a complete misunderstanding of its motivation or from die-hard assimilationism. The program was actually committed to more change and progress toward improved standards of Indian life than had ever been contemplated in the preceding century of Indian affairs. How Indian, in the sense of old Indian ways of life, are the livestock corporations, the farming and husbandry co-operatives, the co-operative tribal stores, or the commercial credit that were essential parts of the Collier program? The program was in fact dedicated to constructive accommodation and adjustment of Indians to modern American life, but also to the idea – unpopular, perhaps, among most Americans – that a decision to become completely assimilated and give up Indian identity and community life was not for the nation or the government to make but for the Indians to make for themselves.

IV

Some Americans see assimilation, and ending Indian communities and special Indian status, as in the best interests of Indians. The legal forms which now safeguard the status of Indian communities are seen as restrictions or limitations of Indian activity and opportunity and not as marks of Indian freedom. The Indian rights of tax exemption on trust property are not ordinarily so characterized, of course; they are usually written off as peculiarities, which set Indians apart from others, increasing social distance and the difficulties of intergroup relations. But such features of the trust situation as government control over the use and disposition of trust-protected Indian lands and other tribal assets are seen as hampering and restrictive, as undue paternalism and overprotection which increase Indian dependency and destroy Indian initiative.

Few would deny that over-paternalism has often impaired the administration of Indian affairs. The trustee relation is often ambiguous and difficult; abuse of power on the one hand or over-anxiety on the other both may have damaging effects.

The difficulty is compounded in Indian affairs because the federal government is in a trustee relation to both communities and individuals. The trust protection of individual property is an outgrowth of the federal trust relation to tribal property; tribal property may be individualized, but individual owners may hold restricted titles (in theory, being judged incompetent), rather than unrestricted titles in fee simple. This trust relation to individuals has all too often involved abuses or over-protection, and it may well be that the relation is more restrictive than liberating, especially if individuals have chosen the path of detribalization and assimilation.

But it is the federal trust relation to Indian communities rather than individuals that is most germane in this discussion.

In the case of communities, it is doubtful that the paternalistic abuses which have occurred are inherent in the federal trust relation. Tribal self-government, for example, since its organization under the IRA, has suffered on a good many occasions from unwarranted government interference. When Indians asked for clarification of their rights under new tribal constitutions, superintendents were often too prone to interpret provisions in favor of their own authority and against that of the tribe. And when graft or corruption is alleged against tribal councils and administration, officials all too often have intervened so eagerly that Indians have had little opportunity to work out democratic processes for themselves. Federal trusteeship can be operated without such abuses.

Perhaps the more important question about the restrictive or liberating character of the protected status of Indian communities is what kind of freedom we are talking about. The freedom of Indians to become as non-Indian and assimilated as they wish cannot be the issue here. The Indians are citizens with the full rights of citizenship, and many have exercised their freedom to become completely Americanized. But there are many who want and need the freedom to be Indian within the framework of America. For them the existence of the community to which they belong is essential to that freedom, and some defined legal status of the community is essential to its continued existence.

The disappearance of our Indian communities by assimilation has a crucial finality that assimilation can never have for other American minorities. Irish, or German, or Scandinavian, or Italian immigrants who become assimilated can still look toward a homeland from which they came, a viable tradition and culture which dignifies their origins. For the Indian, the tribal community is the only carrier of his tradition; if it disintegrates and disappears, his tradition becomes a matter of history, and he loses part of his identity. We are coming to know the importance of this sense of identification with a viable tradition in the meaning of Israel for the American Jew, or of the emergence of free African nations for the American Negro.

There is a tendency for people in the United States to think that we may be coming of age as a people, that now we may be able to accept diversity in our midst without condescension, and that we may be ready to accept as sovereign equals the many peoples, of many races and creeds and cultures, who coexist with us in the complex modern world. Such a liberalism, however, is not yet the American mood in Indian affairs.

While we are unable to rise above assimilationism in our attitude to the Indians, the legal forms which now safeguard their community life and their right to be Indian may be essential. No doubt other forms could be developed by them within the framework of American law, such as, for example, corporate community life without a federal tie, but Indians are unwilling to risk such a change. They hold fast, in the assimilationist mood of America, to the historical status which protects them.

In other respects, however, the Indians are changing and ready for greater changes. Still greatly handicapped by their predominantly rural situation in an industrialized America, they seek technical assistance and training if they can secure these without sacrificing the Indian status they have and want to keep.

Outstanding in the change going on among Indians is the sudden appearance in the last decade of a strong urge for advanced education. Less than two hundred Indians were in college in 1950. Yet by 1959 more than 4,300 were attending colleges and universities, and the number seems likely to continue to increase. This changed attitude toward education, which involves not only the young but their parents and families as well, implies other less obvious changes in Indian attitudes toward their life in America.

Higher education means, of course, that more Indian individuals may choose the path of non-tribal, assimilated life. But it also means that Indian community life will soon be in the hands of a generation of educated Indians. Some communities may choose to disband, with their members going their separate ways; others may want to carry on group life for an indefinite future period. In either case, the decision is likely to be made by informed, educated people, aware of their past and also of their possibilities in America.

Meanwhile, the best we can do, as Felix Cohen once put it, may be "to get out of the way" of the Indians, to stop hampering their efforts to work out their own destiny, and especially to stop trying to make them give up their Indian identity.[19] In a world which may be moving toward greater internationalism, in which we hope that peoples, however diverse, will choose the way of democracy, we cannot avoid the responsibility for a democratic resolution of the American Indian situation. Our attitude toward the Indians, the stubbornest non-conformists among us, may be the touchstone of our tolerance of diversity anywhere.

8   The cultural significance of the Ghost Dance

Few religious movements have been so fortunate in their contemporary chroniclers as the Ghost Dance of 1890 in the sympathetic record of James Mooney (Mooney 1896). In his long historical account and commentary, Mooney enlarged upon earlier movements of similar nature, ghost dance origins and sources, the doctrine, the forms of the dance, its psychological aspects in the trances, the spread of the religion in detail, the local forms of the religion among a number of the tribes, and the actual historical events which brought some tribes into conflict with the government over the doctrine. But Mooney's report was at once so voluminous and full a record, that since its publication there has been a tendency to regard the Ghost Dance as a closed book, finished and forever settled in this definitive treatment.

James Mooney investigated the Ghost Dance at intervals in the years from 1890 to 1893. Of his own work he states that his investigations brought "personal observation and study of the Ghost Dance down to the beginning of 1894" (Mooney 1896:654). In his introductory remarks, Mooney comments that "the investigation . . . might be continued indefinitely, as the dance still exists [in 1896] and is developing new features at every performance" (Mooney 1896:653). Thus Mooney himself recognized that he had not written the final chapter.

And in truth the Ghost Dance, like all vital cultural manifestations, was not, and could not be, an episode that had an arbitrary beginning and an arbitrary close. In human culture, as in human experience, what has come to attention and prominence never disappears. Either it is retained in some form as a part of culture thereafter, or it leaves its impress and influence upon other aspects of culture.

This paper was read at the Annual Meetings of the American Anthropological Association and the American Folk-Lore Society, Andover, Mass., on December 29, 1931. It was published in the *American Anthropologist* 35:108–15. © 1933 the American Anthropological Association. Reproduced by permission. Not for further reproduction.

To measure the pulse of the Ghost Dance movement, Mooney found it necessary to consider the religious revivals of earlier American Indian prophets, demonstrating that no mere arbitrary point could be selected as the beginning of the Ghost Dance. In a passage of his concluding remarks, Mooney called attention to the fact that among some of the tribes which participated in the Ghost Dance, "the Ghost Dance has become a part of the tribal life and is performed at regular intervals" (Mooney 1896:927), indicating that no arbitrary date could be set upon its close. If the Ghost Dance did not suddenly arise, flourish, and disappear, but rather had a natural growth upon the basis of earlier culture in response to cultural needs, and after the excitement of its period of storm and stress settled down to become a more or less integrated part of a newer, changed culture, then Ghost Dance effects are a significant ethnological problem. For if the field ethnologist today is to penetrate to older levels of aboriginal culture, he must attend to the local Ghost Dance and mark off the changes it has caused.

According to James Mooney's concept of the Ghost Dance it was a movement revolt, religiously directed, an attempt to throw off an alien yoke, and recover aboriginal freedom. In the course of that movement, the activities which composed it could not fail to influence directly the rest of culture. I should like to call attention to certain phases of this influence, of how changes which came about were related to the doctrine and to the activities of the dance. While I shall use facts from the Pawnee to illustrate my meaning, I believe that the general bearing of the point of view will be found relevant to the situation among other tribes.

The Ghost Dance spread among American Indian tribes at a time when the final destruction of native culture was well advanced. Perhaps the greatest destructive influence was not so much the influx of white settlers or the consequent appropriation of tribal lands, as the annihilation of the great herds of buffalo. With the disappearance of the buffalo, the economic stability and security of the Indian tribes vanished. In its place came want and hunger. A feeling of desolation which spread among these tribes made them ripe for any message of hope.

The Ghost Dance doctrine brought hope. It promised a destruction of the invading white man, a return of the buffalo and old Indian ways, and a reunion of the Indians and their deceased forebears. The last may well have been a Christian element, as well as the moral precept accompanying it that Indians were not to fight any more, but live together in one great brotherhood. But the sanction for this hope was native to the Indian mind. It was based on the vision, on the direct supernatural experience. In the vision a message came from the deceased, telling the living what to do, telling the living what would happen.

With the destruction of the buffalo and the influx of the white man, Indian ways of life were vanishing. This was clearly the case if we read the Pawnee story aright. The old Pawnee societies had long since ceased to function. Practically all these societies were concerned with war and hunting. Intertribal warfare had been legally eliminated, although of course occasional skirmishes occurred. But the Pawnee steadfastly maintained their treaty obligations and avoided warfare with their ancient enemies, appealing, as in the case of the Sioux massacre of the Pawnee in 1873, to the federal government for redress. In the same way, tribal hunting became a memory. With the disappearance of warfare and hunting, the societies no longer had a function.

The great esoteric bundle ceremonies of the Pawnee had also ceased. The reason given by old men today is not a failure of belief, but the same failure of the supply of buffalo which destroyed many of the societies. A cardinal tenet of Pawnee ideology was the sacred character of buffalo meat. None but buffalo meat could be used in the great ceremonies; in fact, not only was buffalo meat essential, but in many of the bundle ceremonies buffalo concepts and orientations of powers concerned primarily with the buffalo were part and parcel of the ritual and ceremony itself. Without these aspects of the ritual and ceremony, the performance became meaningless.

The medicine men's phase of Pawnee religion had not entirely died out. Many leading doctors who controlled the right to demonstrate dances had died, taking their esoteric teachings with them to the grave; but one or two Doctor Dances were still held almost every year. For these a sufficient supply of buffalo meat could be obtained, or the medicine men themselves found justification for substituting ordinary beef for buffalo meat. The great Doctor Performances involving feats of magic and sleight of hand had ceased. The last one occurred among the Pawnee in 1878 or 1879.

The ordinary social activities of daily life had also broken down to a great extent. Most of the games were no longer played, or were revived here and there intermittently. Thus while in former times the spring was not only a time of great religious and ceremonial activity, of great economic and industrial activity, but also a time for the revival of games for the young and old, in the years before the Ghost Dance there was no general spring revival of social activity.

This decline of Pawnee culture was not altogether a direct result of the changing conditions, but in considerable part was connected with the Pawnee pattern for handing on traditional knowledge.

According to the Pawnee conception, the knowledge and learning of an individual had to be handed down by actual instruction of the young. This was somewhat different for the two basic types of bundles: the sacred bundles (with which can be associated the society bundles, probably derivative), and the doctor bundles. A sacred bundle was physically owned by a man who did not necessarily know its significance and ritual, although he did carry out his obligations toward it according to the instruction of a priest: it was physically cared for by the owner's wife; and its ritual learning was controlled or owned by a priest. The bundle itself was inherited in the male line (ordinarily). The ritual learning was taught by the priest to his successor, usually a close relative (though not necessarily in the male line alone), but lacking close kin of the right temperament and character, the priest taught whom he wished. On the other hand, a medicine man owned his bundle *and* its correlative teachings, performances, rites. He turned these over to his successor, who was usually a close relative (son or nephew, etc.), but again, if the medicine man found his own kin unwilling to take over his bundle, he would teach someone else who came to him desiring to learn.

Ordinarily, a man taught his successor largely by demonstration. That is, the apprentice took part in the actual demonstrations of the ritual, watching what went on. In the course of the procedure, his master explained details. As the teacher found his pupil mastering phases of the activity, he turned over to the pupil such parts of the ritual, performance, etc., as he found were understood. In this way, as a rule, a man learned *all* of another's teachings only if the teacher lived to be an old man. In fact, the Pawnee conception was that as a man taught what he knew he gave up part of his life, and that when he had given over all his teachings, he would die. Hence the old and learned always held back something until they were ready to die. If a priest or medicine man died, what he had not taught to his successor was lost. Usually, when an old man knew he was on his deathbed, and valued his learning and his apprentice, he called the apprentice in, and in dying whispers told him the essentials of what he had not before that time communicated. Now since among the Pawnee a man has no right to handle in a ceremonial manner what he does not understand, what he has not learned to carry out, it happened in most cases that doctor bundles were broken up upon death of the owner. Some part of the bundle had already been transferred to the medicine man's apprentice; some further part which the apprentice understood but had not already been given, was now handed over to him; and the rest was buried with the deceased medicine man. As the ownership of the sacred bundles was divorced from the knowledge of their rituals, the same did not happen to them. The physical bundle survived, but gradually less and less of its contents were understood by living men.

The important point to remember in this is that in old Pawnee ideology what of traditional learning was lost through death was lost beyond recovery. There was no sanction for carrying out any ritual, other than that the one who attempted to carry it out had learned about it from the man who formerly had controlled it and demonstrated it.

As conditions became unfavorable for carrying out the activities and demonstrating the rituals of the ceremonies and societies, there was neither the stimulus for the old to teach and for the young to learn, nor the customary mechanism in operation for the transfer of learning. Hence the normal rate of cultural forgetting was accelerated, and in the course of only a few years, relatively, most of the old traditional ways were buried in the grave.

Into this situation of cultural decay and gradual darkness, the Ghost Dance doctrine shone like a bright light. Indian ways were not gone, never to be recovered. Indian ways were coming back. Those who had lived before in the "golden age" were still carrying on old ceremonies, old dances, old performances, and old games in the beyond. They were coming back; they were bringing the old ways and the buffalo. Dance, dance, dance. The white man would be destroyed by a great wind. The Indian would be left with the buffalo, with his ancestors, with his old friends and his old enemies. Cast aside the white man's ways like an old garment; put on the clothes of the Indian again. Get ready for the new day and the old times.

The dancers shook and fell in hypnotic trances. They saw the people in the beyond dancing too. They saw them playing games, ring and pole games, hand games; they saw them gathering for war dances and the hunt; they saw them gathered in their old society brotherhoods.

The visionaries awoke and told what they saw. *They* are doing all these things; we must too. So the people began games and dances. They revived war dances and societies; they revived the Horn Dance, the Young Dog Dance, the Iruska, the Big Horse Society, the Roached Heads, the Crazy Dogs. Again they carried out the Pipe Dance; they renewed interest in the Doctor Dances. They played hand games.

In short, the activity of the Ghost Dance times was not a mere revival of old ways, it became a renaissance of Pawnee culture.

This effect occurred in the following way: In a vision the subject would "see" some old way of life which had come to be disregarded. He would "remember" it. His vision then became a command upon those alive who knew how it must be carried out, to do so. Sometimes there were men alive who knew the thing thoroughly and were persuaded by the demand of such a supernatural message to begin it again. But often a ritual or dance was only partially remembered. Then many men would get together and pool their memories to revive the affair. If the "seen" phase of old life was social and non-esoteric, the visionary himself would revive the old way. Hence games, and hand games.

Most important of all were revivals of those old ways which had been utterly lost. In older Pawnee theory, as we saw, only direct learning from the owner sanctioned use and demonstration. But in a vision in the Ghost Dance one saw the deceased (the "ghost," in other words); one saw those who had known how to do these things and had died without handing them on. The deceased in the vision told the visionary what to do just as he would have done in life. He appealed to the visionary to revive his ways because the old life was soon to reappear in its entirety. Thus an entirely new form of sanction came into Pawnee thought. Where it would have been sacrilege formerly to have carried out a dance or ceremony to which one had no right, where before such behavior would have invited supernatural punishment, the trance vision now constituted a supernatural command that the performance *be* revived.[20]

This renaissance meant not only the revival of activities. It meant also that a good deal of ceremonial paraphernalia which had been lost or buried in times past, was duplicated from memory and vision. Many of the society regalia and ritual objects which were purchased by the museums around 1900 from the Pawnee were not the old sacred objects. Those had long before disappeared, many of them prior to the movement of the Pawnee to Oklahoma in 1874–76. They were the Ghost Dance revival objects, the Ghost Dance reincarnations of the old lances, drums, regalia, and pipes.

Following this revival of old ways, there was a new reintegration of Ghost Dance suggestions, old ways, and current thought. In terms of this the Ghost Dance hand games arose, and passed through many transformations. In some of these, special revivals of old societies were incorporated. New forms of intertribal visiting were founded on revivals of old customs and Ghost Dance ideas. Society and dance revivals were integrated with Ghost Dance thought. Thus vital phases of Pawnee life which survived until recent years were not exactly what Pawnee life had been in the nineteenth century; they were based on old forms and traditions, but they were changed permanently into new forms by the cultural stimulant of the Ghost Dance years.

The Ghost Dance was not merely a religious revival movement. Its roots lie deep in the gradual cultural destruction which preceded it. Its doctrine and the activities it demanded infused new life into the culture, and constituted instrumentalities for an actual renaissance of the forms of old culture. Along with this renaissance there came into being also new cultural forms, unknown before.

9   Foreword to *The Pawnee Ghost Dance Hand Game*

I

The Pawnee Ghost Dance Hand Game was written in 1932, based on field research among the Pawnees in 1929–31. It was first published in 1933 by the Columbia University Press as a volume in its series of Columbia University Publications in Anthropology.

My field research in the 1930s was primarily devoted to intensive study of traditional Pawnee religion, in which I had an opportunity to use for descriptive detail a large manuscript by James R. Murie and Clark Wissler entitled "Ceremonies of the Pawnee," then awaiting publication by the Bureau of American Ethnology. With this in hand, I could largely disregard recording descriptive ritual detail and concentrate on understanding Pawnee theology and philosophy. It was while I did this day after day with many informants that I discovered the tremendous impact of the Ghost Dance doctrines of the 1890s on the Pawnee people, and the creative emergence in those years of the Pawnee Ghost Dance Hand Games. Postponing work on the traditional religious theology in the expectation that the Murie-Wissler manuscript would be published shortly, I wrote my first book to tell the story of the Ghost Dance years and the Pawnee Ghost Dance Hand Games. Publication of the "Ceremonies of the Pawnee" unfortunately languished for these many years. Only now or in another year, with special linguistic editing by Douglas R. Parks, is the Smithsonian Institution expected to publish it.[21]

It was possible in 1929–31 to recapture events of the 1890s because a great deal about Ghost Dance times was known and remembered by Pawnees of those years. It would be impossible to do this study today among living Pawnees.

This chapter was originally published as the Author's Foreword to Alexander Lesser, *The Pawnee Ghost Dance Hand Game*, pp. ix–xxiv. © 1978 The Board of Regents of the University of Wisconsin System. Reproduced by permission of The University of Wisconsin Press.

The book showed that the Ghost Dance was more than a period of religious excitement for the Pawnee. Its doctrines and activities involved individuals, families, and traditional groups in efforts to remember and carry out again traditional ways that were on the verge of extinction. The Ghost Dance was a *nativistic* revival. Its reassertion of Pawnee values was an experience of Pawnee ethnic identity – a renewed awareness for some, a new experience for others. In our time, ethnic identity, often with goals of political autonomy, is being reasserted by submerged, repressed peoples in many parts of the world. In relation to this widespread phenomenon, the Ghost Dance of years ago among the Pawnee and other Indian Americans can now be understood as the same kind of reassertion of ethnic identity. In fact, it now raises a fundamental question: Is not this the meaning of *any* nativistic revival which occurs under nationalistic assimilation programs of dominant peoples?

The excitement of the Ghost Dance years among the Pawnee continued into the early twentieth century. Indian Affairs officials were concerned in those years to quiet down, if possible, Pawnee Ghost Dance activities, and especially the playing of Ghost Dance Hand Games; they wanted to continue the allotting of land units to individuals and the persuading of Pawnee families to settle on their allotments and farm them. That was the program of assimilation with which Pawnee Ghost Dance excitement interfered.

By the 1930s, when I was among the Pawnee, most revivals of traditional forms were gone again. Life in and around Pawnee, Oklahoma, provided no meaningful basis for sacred bundles and rituals or for men's military societies, and few of the traditional personnel to carry them out survived. The Hand Games lost their religious meaning and became occasions for fun and recreation. They still are in 1977. But the tribal sense of being Pawnees, of having values of their own, of having a history, a language, and traditions from a remote past, remained. In fact, during years of change, from the 1930s to the present, some events have strengthened the Pawnees in their tribalism and in their tribal pride.

The Pawnee population in 1930 was 844, up from its all-time low of 600 in 1900. Actually, the population was steadily increasing, year by year. It numbered 977 in 1938, the year in which the Pawnees established their present tribal organization under the Indian Reorganization Act of the 1934 Indian "New Deal." By 1940 the Pawnee roll was 1,017; and in 1964, 1,898 Pawnees shared in the per capita distribution of a judgment recovered by the tribe from the United States through the Indian Claims Commission. It compensated for inequities in nineteenth-century treaty settlements for their former lands in Kansas and Nebraska. Today, in 1976–77, there are 2,213 Pawnees on the tribal roll.

Although Pawnee life is still related to the town of Pawnee and the county of Pawnee, the relationship has changed fundamentally over the years. In 1930 virtually all Pawnees lived in or near the town, perhaps three-fourths of the 844 members of the tribe within a radius of four or five miles, visiting town constantly by horse and wagon. On Saturdays the town square around the courthouse was a gathering place for families who came to spend a good part of the day, and many walked about in the main streets throughout the day, meeting one another. The official Pawnee Agency of the Bureau of Indian Affairs was at that time about a mile out of town on tribal-owned land.

In contrast to the 1930s, by 1967 less than one-fourth of the tribe lived near Pawnee. Today, in 1977, Pawnee families are much more widely dispersed than ever, and the town itself is no longer a tribal center. On weekends it is as deserted by Pawnees as it is by others. Saturdays are no time to meet people in town, and on Sundays everything in town is closed, including eating places.

Several factors account for this change. The car is one. Increased education and technical training of Pawnees have led any number of families to live where they find jobs and career opportunities. A good many live in other Oklahoma towns and the cities of Oklahoma City and Tulsa. Many Pawnees live outside the state, numbers in the Southwest and California.

The political situation is the most striking factor in the changed political relationship of Pawnees to the town and to themselves as a tribe. The Bureau of Indian Affairs Pawnee Agency, which manages the Bureau affairs of five tribes – the Ponca, Oto, Kaw, and Tonkawa, besides the Pawnee – formerly located on Pawnee lands out of town, is now in Pawnee itself, in rented quarters. The Pawnee Tribe, by contrast, as a phase of its steadily developing tribal self-government, conducts most of its business in a Pawnee Tribal Business Building on Pawnee tribal land in the area where the Agency once was. Both the Pawnee Agency and the Pawnee Tribal Office are open weekdays only.

For recreational gatherings larger than families-at-home, the Pawnee reserve lands out of town provide facilities, some in use and more being developed. There are camp grounds and fair grounds, and room for the annual July pow-wow, considered by many Pawnees, even families living at a distance, an annual homecoming.

The changes have made the Pawnees less and less concerned with the town of Pawnee. The tribe is thinking today much more in terms of itself, of the tribal center developing on Pawnee lands, including the Pawnee Tribal Business Building and the Pawnee Hospital, already operating, the Round House recreation center in process, a Pawnee Industrial Park, well advanced in planning, renovated housing, and many other projects already part of tribal approved plans.

In the early 1930s the Pawnee tribe was not organized politically. The tradition of hereditary chiefs provided a mechanism still respected by Pawnees, and the chiefs acted for the people in dealing with United States officials. When the Indian New Deal of President Roosevelt's administration offered for the first time, in the Indian Reorganization Act (IRA) and supplementary legislation, a nonassimilation program in Indian Affairs, the Pawnee supported it early. The program accepted the existence of Indian communities and attempted to provide them with the legal status and machinery and the economic resources needed to continue their tribal existence as long as they chose. Tribal self-government and tribal business corporations were authorized, and provisions were made for an adequate land base, financial credit, and adequate training and education.

The Pawnees began drafting a plan for a tribal constitution in 1936, although they could not adopt it until 1937 when the Oklahoma Indian Welfare Act became part of the IRA body of legislation; the original IRA did not include Oklahoma tribes. In the draft, the traditional status of Pawnee chiefs was recognized by establishing a Chiefs Council as one of two governing bodies of the tribe. In January 1938, the Pawnees voted to adopt the proposed Tribal Constitution and By-Laws. Their support was substantial. Of 460 eligible to vote, 257 (56 percent) participated and voted 197 to 60 (3.5 to 1) in favor of the plan. A Pawnee Tribal Business Council of eight members was established, to be elected every two years by vote of all Pawnees twenty-one years old or older, and a Nasharo or Chiefs Council of eight, to be elected every four years. Chiefs could not be members of the Business Council, and only chiefs, with inherited rights of chieftainship, were eligible for election to the Nasharo Council. The Business Council was to be the active governing body of the tribe, to speak and act and transact tribal business for the tribe, and to appoint subordinate functionaries. The Nasharo Council had the right to review all Business Council actions concerned with tribal membership and tribal claims and rights under treaties. All tribesmembers were guaranteed full rights of citizenship under the United States and Oklahoma constitutions. Although men and women voted, only men were initially eligible for positions on the Business Council; a constitutional amendment making both men and women twenty-five years old or older eligible was ratified December 17, 1974.

In its structure and principles, and in the spirit of the Indian Reorganization Act behind it, the 1938 Pawnee Indian tribal organization was a further step in the realization of Pawnee identity. It strengthened tribal confidence and pride. It offered a framework on which Pawnees could structure an improved life and a Pawnee future.

First, of course, the Pawnees, like other tribes organized under the IRA, had to learn the ordinary day-by-day business of operating government agencies of their own, of all the details of budgeting, managing funds and paying bills, hiring and firing, and complicated routines of programming and making decisions and plans that could become realities. In all this, which had for so many years been handled by the Commissioner of Indian Affairs, the Bureau of Indian Affairs, and their local Pawnee officialdom, the Pawnees found that they could not exercise tribal authority freely. There were strong habits not easily shaken of turning to the Agency for advice and decisions; and, on the other side, the Bureau of Indian Affairs and its representatives were not able to end automatically their practice of running the lives and business of Pawnee individuals and the Pawnee Tribe. Learning by doing was difficult under these conditions.

But a larger difficulty for the Pawnee Tribe, from 1938 to the late 1950s, was that the philosophy and the principles of the IRA did not have steady majority support in Congress, and after Roosevelt's administration, in the Executive Branch. Quite the opposite. The view that assimilation of the American Indians should be the goal in Indian Affairs remained a commitment of many, and legislative enactments and resolutions, as well as executive actions, expressed that repeatedly.

In the early 1950s, for example, the Commissioner and Bureau of Indian Affairs promoted a program of relocation of reservation Indians into urban centers. The theory was that Indian areas, predominantly rural, could not be developed to support their Indian population, that these areas were in fact overpopulated. Even if unskilled, Indians should be helped to find jobs in and settle in industrial areas. Those who did, it was expected, would leave Indian reservation life behind and prefer to live permanently in cities as part of the American labor force. The program opposed any plans, by Indian tribes or others, to bring industry or business onto Indian-owned lands and thereby create new economic opportunities for Indians at home. In the end, the relocation program proved a relatively weak threat to Indian tribal existence or development; it failed to achieve its goals. Most Indians who were persuaded to try relocation, unskilled as they were and offered virtually no technical training, met unemployment in the cities if it occurred by returning home to rejoin their kinfolk.

More threatening to Indian community development and even to the continued existence of IRA tribal organization was the commitment of Congress in the mid-1950s to a program for termination of federal responsibility for Indians as rapidly as possible. The theory behind this, given support even in some anthropological studies, was that it was the federal status of Indian tribes which was responsible for their continuing separateness and rejection of assimilation – a federal status which went back to colonial times when colonists made treaties with Indian tribes as they found them, autonomous and self-governing. House Concurrent Resolution 108 put into words the congressional determination to terminate the federal status and rights of Indian tribes, and for years it was quoted as a national commitment by assimilationists in Congress and in the Bureau of Indian Affairs. Indian tribal opposition to termination, along with the strong support of public organizations concerned with Indian rights and liberal members of Congress, was not able to prevent all legislative termination efforts. After general termination legislation was defeated, the Congress shrewdly adopted a course of enacting termination bills tribe by tribe, multiplying the difficulties of opposing them. Some tribes were terminated despite powerful opposition, including, in 1954, such notable cases as the Klamath Indians of Oregon and the Menomini Indians of Wisconsin. The Menomini case proved so conclusively a failure after a few years that the Menominis and their friends were able, in 1973, to get their status reversed and return the tribe to federal status and jurisdiction.

The Pawnee Tribe was not directly attacked by termination legislation. Assimilationists did not claim that the Pawnees were "ready" for such a drastic change. Even for assimilationists, to be "ready" meant more advanced economic development than the Pawnee Tribe had yet achieved. But termination as a threat and the practical obstructions of tribal self-government by bureaucratic Bureau of Indian Affairs paternalism continued. They were actually ended only in the 1960s by a fundamental change in national Indian policy. Termination was put aside or conceptually postponed, with the thought that economic development and improvement of Indian life with federal help must precede any idea of ending Indian federal status.

The 1960s, under President Kennedy and President Johnson, were years marked by a national recognition of widespread chronic unemployment, poverty, poor housing, and poor health, especially among deprived minority groups, and equally marked was a determination to do something about such conditions. A whole body of corrective legislation was enacted, dealing with area redevelopment, public housing, a youth conservation corps, the war on poverty, civil rights. New in the history of Indian

Affairs was the inclusion of Indian communities among minorities to be helped by these programs (see Schifter 1970). A good many involved Indian Americans with government agencies or departments other than the Interior Department and its Bureau of Indian Affairs (traditionally their only jurisdiction). Prominent among these new jurisdictions were the Department of Commerce, the Department of Labor, and the Department of Health, Education, and Welfare. In some cases also, new federal directives added new obligations toward Indian Americans to the responsibilities of the Bureau of Indian Affairs.

The new opportunities in all areas required a procedure new to most tribes. Grants or loans, to be secured for approved purposes, called for applications, often complex and varying from case to case, made directly by recognized government units to appropriate agencies. The organized Pawnee Tribe was a recognized local government unit. But in understanding requirements and procedures, the tribe had virtually no experience, and little or no preparation by education or technical training. In a few cases, Congress tried to provide that needed experts from Washington visit Indians to help. But more frequently, even to make initial program applications, Pawnees found it necessary to send delegates to Washington for help. It took a good many years, especially as additional federal programs developed, to learn by trial and error, and only in the 1970s had the Pawnee Tribal Business Council reached a mature degree of outlook and performance.

This maturity appears in a devotion to Pawnee needs and goals shown by the core of tribal leadership: improvement of economic conditions and opportunities, education, health, and the Pawnee future as Pawnees get their continuing attention. When the American Indian Movement (AIM) enlisted Pawnee adherents and led a protest in Pawnee, Oklahoma, in 1972, the tribe looked beyond AIM's pan-Indian philosophy and action methods, and any important influence of AIM was short-lived. Most Pawnees saw the Pawnee future in Pawnee ethnic terms, different in important ways from a generalized pan-Indian American movement, requiring separate and independent planning on its own. The Pawnee Tribal Business Council concerned itself even more intensely with education and technical training for immediate and future opportunities, with economic planning to improve conditions of Pawnee individual, family, and tribal life, with social planning for better recreation and enjoyment for all, and with cultural possibilities of holding and recovering Pawnee ethnic history and the Pawnee language.

Education has been and is vital to individual and tribal development in dealing with the alien, non-Indian world. Special technical training for technical jobs is of course chosen by many. But others, and their number is increasing, elect to study at advanced institutions along professional and career lines. This trend somewhat parallels the needs of the Pawnees for specialized experts and long-term thinking.

By 1976–77, virtually all Pawnee children were finishing public school. This has meant that an increased number have gone on to public high school, and today, according to the chairman of the town school board, 95 percent of Pawnees in high school complete their studies and graduate. Perhaps a third of the high school graduates go on further into advanced technical training or into college. Informed estimates are that thirty to sixty Pawnees were enrolled in 1975, 1976, and 1977 at institutions of higher education.

Among college majors, behavioral sciences – sociology and social work, psychology, educational counseling – along with business and law, are increasingly popular. Many women have chosen nursing as a career. Short-courses in mechanics and welding have been popular among men, in clerical skills and cosmetology among women. Clerical work has usually been with the local agency of the Bureau of Indian Affairs or other BIA offices, or with the tribal administration. The Tribal Business Council sets up additional opportunities when it can. For example, in May 1975 the Council contracted with the Bureau of Indian Affairs for an instructor to train tribal employees in bookkeeping, payroll procedures, state and federal withholding taxes, and the like, and in June of that year arranged through the Comprehensive Employment Training Act (CETA) for five on-the-job training openings: three security officers, a jailor, and a cook.

Financial help for education, a vital factor in the Pawnee educational development that has occurred, is increasingly available through government agencies. A Higher Educational Grant Program through HEW has assisted high school students for many years; these grants are at most $1400 a year. For the past four years Basic Educational Opportunity Grants, based on need, have supplemented HEW grants for high school and beyond. Loan programs, more widely available, have helped Indians and non-Indians alike. Short vocational technical training courses, usually at Indian Meridian in Stillwater, get CETA assistance. College work is principally at Oklahoma State University, but other Oklahoma institutions are attended as well. In summary, Pawnee Indians are now making use of the whole range of public schools and high schools, trade schools, colleges, and universities.

Although general economic conditions have improved over the years since the 1930s, Pawnee Indians are still, in 1977, a poor people. Income of individuals and families is primarily from land rented to non-Indian farmers, supplemented by income of those who work. Few have business enterprises of their own in Pawnee or elsewhere. Many skilled and professional Pawnees live and work away from the Pawnee area. Pawnee, Oklahoma, offers limited employment for Indians, principally through the Bureau Agency or the Pawnee Tribe itself. The town of Pawnee is a declining area economically. The development of Stillwater, about thirty miles away, as the University of Oklahoma center with a student population of 10,000 to 15,000, and as a commercial and industrial center, has made Pawnee and its commercial activities peripheral, showing few signs of business progress over the past forty years. The non-Indian residential area of Pawnee has grown considerably, as many who work or do business in Stillwater live in Pawnee and commute, but business has shrunken.

Unemployment among Pawnees has been and is high. In 1967, Pawnee median income in the Pawnee area was about three-fourths of that of local non-Indians, and the latter was low. A 1972 survey showed that more than 50 percent of the potential Pawnee labor force was unemployed. In 1977 unemployment is considered to be as high as 75 percent, and as having been more than 60 percent over the last several years. The Pawnees are, of course, eligible for social security programs, and the unemployed have recourse to unemployment insurance. But the economic needs of the area and of the Pawnees are obvious, and the tribal leadership is deeply concerned with this in tribal programming.

The efforts of the Pawnee Tribal Business Council to manage Pawnee affairs effectively and to promote Pawnee development are supported, even financially, by present federal policy. The Bureau of Indian Affairs administers a Tribal Government Development Program under which the Business Council can make contracts for needed personnel and equipment, and an Office of Native American Programs (ONAP) in Washington funds special tribal program needs, including employment of required specialists. Under the latter, the Pawnee Tribe added to its active staff certified public accountants, an engineer, an attorney, and a program specialist, as well as necessary secretaries for them. The tribal attorney completed action last year which added to the tribal reserve forty acres of Pawnee land that had come under the control of the town of Pawnee. In legal action with the Arkansas Riverbed Trust Authority, he recovered for the Pawnee the value of their interest in the Arkansas and Cimarron riverbeds. The engineer helped the Pawnee plan construction projects and determine site locations for future construction. And for special help, the tribe was able in 1977 to ask BIA land specialists to appraise all Pawnee tribal land, and to turn to the Oklahoma Indian Affairs Commission for assistance in preparing a Comprehensive Land Use and Economic Resource Plan.

Health and housing developments are a steady part of Tribal Business Council discussions and planning. The tribe is trying to keep the Pawnee Indian Hospital exclusively Pawnee, and in long-range planning seeks to establish a new health center on the Pawnee tribal reserve, to provide comprehensive health services. In housing, the Pawnee Tribal Housing Authority, established under the United States Public Housing Administration, is planning, where possible, rehabilitation of old housing on the tribal reserve (once offices and homes of BIA teachers and officials), and planned in 1977 to build twenty-five new low-rent housing units.

Different proposals, submitted as separate units to appropriate agencies for funding, require that the tribe have an overall development program in mind into which each proposal fits as a part. Such a program was drafted in December 1975 and discussed by the Business Council in the early months of 1976. It states in an integrated way the series of numbered and titled projects which, taken together, are visualized by the Pawnees today as their way to achieve progress toward better Pawnee individual and tribal life. As proposed, it is known as the Pawnee Heritage Program. Its project themes are Heritage House, Elders Council Center, Youth Council Center, Job Opportunities Office, and Pawnee Tribal Finance Office.

The Elders and Youth Council centers virtually describe themselves. Each proposes a facility for an age group, to provide a broad range of services. There are 30 to 50 elderly Pawnees now served meals twice a month at the Pawnee Tribal Community House; the project envisages staffing a facility for 30 to 100 elderly Pawnees who live in and around Pawnee County. It would provide, besides nutrition, continuing education, health services, and needed transportation, recreation, and counseling. The Youth Center would service 150 Pawnees now twelve to eighteen years of age. Besides sports facilities and equipment, it would provide supplemental education, counseling, and training in leadership and community services. Both programs were visualized as requiring a year to be ready to begin operation.

The Job Opportunities Office, the Finance Office, and the Industrial Park Authority, taken together, constitute a fundamental economic development program. The Industrial Park on the Pawnee reserve is designed to bring new industries into the tribal world, with new employment for Pawnees; they would have the competitive advantage of paying no state or local taxes. The Job Office is to provide information on skills needed for the new employment to come; and the Finance Office is to develop a program to meet all the fiscal needs of individuals, small businesses, and new industries.

Heritage House is the most ambitious and idealistic of the projects. It is conceived as a centralizing force for the tribal organization, the Youth Center, the Elders Center, and the Pawnee people at large. It would provide a museum for the Pawnee cultural and historical heritage, and facilities and staff for bilingual, bicultural, and supplemental education. Its major subject areas are language, art, music and dance, and tribal history. It is central to the overall program effort to develop Pawnee confidence and pride of origin, to strengthen motivations and drives toward Pawnee self-determination.

By 1977 only a few parts of the bold Heritage Program were achieved, or in progress, or fully approved. The most prominent achievement was the building of a Pawnee Administration Building on tribal land by renovation of the old Indian School. A grant of $300,000 from the Economic Development Administration (EDA) met most of the cost; work was begun in mid-1976 for completion by January 1977. The exterior was finished and about one-third of the interior rooms, and in 1977 the Pawnee Tribal Business Council was working in its own modern quarters. The original plan was to relocate the entire Bureau of Indian Affairs Agency – now in rented office space in Pawnee – in the large facilities of the new Pawnee Administration Building. The Pawnee planned to finance the work of completing the interior for the BIA with EDA loans, and expected to carry the loans with the rent to be paid by the BIA. This plan is at an impasse, because the other tribes serviced by the BIA Agency – the Ponca, Oto, Kaw, and Tonkawa – claim the right to share in the BIA rent payments. The Pawnee Tribe, which owns the land and building and would be responsible for the EDA loans, denies any legal right of others to share the rents. Despite this situation, the Pawnee Tribe is extremely proud of its achievement and of its own Pawnee Tribal Business Building, the center of Pawnee self-government and business activity now. Pawnee officials must, on occasion, meet with Agency officials in town; but there are important Pawnee business occasions when Agency officials have to join Pawnee officials at the new Pawnee offices.

The Pawnee Industrial Park has made important headway in planning but in 1977 is not as yet funded. The Pawnees report that two industrial concerns want to locate in the Park. According to Pawnee projections, these, if successful, could provide employment for as many as 600 in three to four years. Such a development is seen as primary by Pawnee leaders, who consider improved economic conditions and reduction of Pawnee unemployment a precondition for all other goals. But a strong desire among the people for more immediate satisfactions gave a recreation center, the Round House as central to the camp grounds, greater priority. By 1977 it had been approved and work had begun. Tradition in fact won in its design – round and built of wood, instead of oblong and made of metal, the latter preferable from a technical viewpoint.

The language program made a beginning in 1977. The Pawnee language had been described as gradually disappearing. A 1974 count showed 190 speakers, most of them over forty years of age. The plan of the program began in September 1977 by recording the speech and songs of older Pawnees. It looks toward the preparation of a bilingual source book, and the stated goal is the teaching of Pawnee in school, and in the end bilingual, bicultural education for all age groups. Most important, it is understood in discussions among Pawnee leaders as a program that can bring young and old together in reviving what is almost a lost part of Pawnee culture.

The Pawnee language program, with other commitments of the Heritage House plan, reaffirms the continuing determination of many Pawnees to maintain Pawnee identity into the future. The past fifty years of Pawnee life, despite the confusions and changes of federal Indian policy over the years, are putting assimilation and loss of Indianism aside and structuring Pawnee definition of Pawnee individual and tribal destiny.

To add a subjective note of personal observation: Talking with Pawnee adults in 1977 was a different experience from that of 1930. Today, Pawnees seemed ready and eager to raise questions about Pawnee origins and history and to expect help in finding answers. Individuals spoke of themselves as Pawnee Indians with a deep pride that seems new and that I had not found in them years ago.

II

In the perspective of the many years since *The Pawnee Ghost Dance Hand Game* was written, it was and is unique and in important ways ahead of its time. The study of culture change among Indian Americans was considered at the time to be primarily a description and analysis of how Indian people had adapted to the white man's superior technology and ways of life. In acculturation, when two peoples of different culture met, there was a giving of culture between them and a receiving of culture. But, in the case of the Indian Americans, the culture of European peoples who met them was assumed to be the giving culture, that of the Indian Americans the receiving culture. *The Pawnee Ghost Dance Hand Game* rejected this view and showed that in the conquest of Indian peoples by Europeans, the colonialism and nationalism of the Europeans made the *assimilation* of the aborigines, for purposes of exploitation, the primary European concern. Assimilation meant that the Indianism of the engulfed peoples would be wiped out, the Indians would become like others of the American population. This study of the Pawnees showed that the Ghost Dance revival movement was a vigorous rejection of the fate that assimilation had in store for the Indians, and the summary of what has happened during the decades since the original study is continuing proof of that interpretation.

In later years it became evident that the rejection of assimilation shown in this study was not exceptional but was characteristic of most Indian American peoples. I summarized the facts in a paper which has become best known under the title "The Right Not to Assimilate" [Chapter 7].

The Pawnee Ghost Dance Hand Game showed, however, more than rejection of assimilation, as I pointed out in the beginning of this foreword. The Ghost Dance years among the Pawnee were a time of reassertion of Pawnee values, a revival of Indianism and Indian identity. During decades of the twentieth century, the Pawnee tribe has maintained the essentials of that Indianism and takes pride today in being Pawnee. This case, as I have pointed out, raises the broad general question of whether any nativistic revival under such assimilation conditions is not a reassertion of native identity.

The Pawnee Ghost Dance revival was a time not only of excitement but of joy. After the sadness and losses of nineteenth-century Pawnee experience, the 1890s inspired among the Pawnees a revival of play, of games. Intertwined with their faith in a new coming of old ways and a return of their lost kin was a happiness that made their old games new experiences to enjoy. The Hand Games, based on a traditional men's gambling game, became sacred ceremonies for men, women, and children, and today, no longer rituals, the games are played for fun and recreation.

The empirical method of study and presentation, with Pawnee history and traditions as an integral part of the context, made the analysis of the Hand Games an exceptional opportunity to achieve an understanding of Pawnee ritualism. The traditional Pawnee ceremonies are complex and involve an intricate interweaving of symbols in their formal offerings. In the Hand Game rituals the powers involved are limited, although the ritual formalism followed is consistent with traditional procedures. It was therefore possible to reduce the forms in the Hand Games to the limited abstraction basic to all Pawnee rituals. Moreover, the comparison of the several offerings – the tobacco and smoke offerings and the food offerings – showed that the order and form of the offering with pipe and tobacco was the definitive structure of other offerings in the same ritual; so that the handling of the pipe, when analyzed, proved the key to the entire ritual. In the study of Doctor Dances in the 1930s, along with other traditional ceremonies, this discovery of structure in the Hand Games proved true in the traditional forms. In this sense, the Hand Game study was and remains an important contribution to the study of Pawnee religion in all its complexity, and I believe to the analysis of ritual in general.

The most important contribution of *The Pawnee Ghost Dance Hand Game*, however, is methodological. This was recognized in its initial review in the *American Anthropologist* by William Duncan Strong, who wrote, "This study is a forceful demonstration 'of the inevitability of founding ethnological methodology on a metaphysic of history'"(Strong 1936:112–13). In the book itself I wrote that it was an "illustrative case" in terms of which "I would contend that methodologically, time perspective or historicity is essential to an understanding of culture, whatever special approach is undertaken. Culture is not a static content but a dynamic continuum like the rest of the universe. Its state at any moment, like the condition of any element within it, has multitudinous associations, affects and effects, and has been determined by many factors of which the greater part have not determinately but accidentally come to play a part." A footnote added, "From the standpoint taken herein functionalism in social anthropology which is divorced from time perspective is metaphysically false" [Lesser 1978:336].

Functionalism, with a denial of the relevance of history to an understanding of functional relations within culture, was at that time becoming an insistent approach in ethnology and anthropology. Two years after *The Pawnee Ghost Dance Hand Game* was written, with that study and other data as a basis, I challenged the antihistorical functional position in a paper read at joint sessions of the American Folk-Lore Society and Section H of the American Association for the Advancement of Science. In it, basing my view on the meaning of functional relations in mathematics and the natural sciences, I stated that "a genuinely functional relation is one which is established between two or more terms or variables such that it can be asserted that under certain defined conditions . . . certain determined expressions of those conditions . . . are observed" (Lesser 1935:392 [Chapter 3]). To indicate the way in which time perspective is essential to establish such functional relations, I offered a description of the meaning of history in the study of culture, as follows:

We see such and such events going on. Many things are always happening at the same time, however. How are we to determine whether or not those things which happen at the same time are related to one another? For it is obvious that they may be contemporary events, or even serial events, not because they are related to one another but because their determinants, unknown and unobserved, have caused them to happen at the same or subsequent times. In short, contemporary or associated events may be merely coexistences. Culture, at any one time, is first and foremost a mass of coexistent events. If we are to attempt to define relationships between such events it is impossible in view of the known historicity of things, to assume that the relations lie on the contemporary surface of events. Whatever occurs is determined more by events which happened prior to the occasion in question than by what can be observed contemporaneously with it. As soon as we turn to prior events for an understanding of events observed, we are turning to history. History is no more than that. It is a utilization of the conditioning fact of historicity for the elucidation of seen events (Lesser 1935:392 [Chapter 3]).

In a lengthy discussion which followed my presentation, A. R. Radcliffe-Brown, a prominent functionalist, took issue with my position, and many rose to defend it. Among them, William Duncan Strong, in his remarks, called attention to my *Pawnee Ghost Dance Hand Game* as an empirical study in which I had demonstrated the reality and validity of my thesis. In a publication in which Radcliffe-Brown was invited to summarize his comments on my paper, he said in a foreword, which has never been republished with his article: "I do not define 'function' in the same way as Dr. Lesser. In the circumstances I cannot offer any real criticism of his paper" (Radcliffe-Brown 1935:394).

Nonhistorical functionalism is associated with studies of peoples and cultures which are presented *as if* a cross section of time – a single moment in the stream of time – had been captured and put on paper. Such ethnologies describe a people or a culture without recognition of its existence in time and place, or of its relations with other peoples. The result is a picture or a configuration that is false to reality. The concept which has been used for such studies is that they are *synchronic*, analyses of pure contemporaneity, and they are distinguished from studies which take the historical context into account by calling the latter *diachronic*. It is an essential meaning of *The Pawnee Ghost Dance Hand Game* that the distinction between synchronic and diachronic is artificial and makes no contribution to the study of human cultures and human history or evolution. Any attempt at synchronic analysis inevitably leads the analyst into considerations of diachronic data that are relevant; and any attempt at purely diachronic analysis leads inevitably into relevant synchronic relations. The synchronic–diachronic distinction cannot define different kinds of ethnological studies. Every study, to be true to fact and to include what is relevant to thorough understanding, is of necessity both synchronic and diachronic at the same time.

10   Anthropology and the future of internationalism

As an undergraduate at Columbia College in 1920, I began the study of anthropology with Professor Franz Boas. Ever since, I have been inspired by his spirit and his faith that empirical science, especially through the study of mankind itself, can contribute to the solutions of the great problems of mankind. It is in this spirit that I shall attempt to relate insights of anthropology to some contemporary problems, problems of global human affairs critical in the present and crucial for the human future.

My plan in outline is simple. First, I propose to refer briefly to internationalization, and to the signs around us that – at least in the long run – it is increasing. I will add in summary historical and anthropological background on the evolution of that trend in intergroup human affairs. In doing so, I hope to point out some of the institutional defects we inherit from the past – defects that prevent contemporary internationalism from contributing more toward the achievement of a peaceful global life. Second, I want to try to draw on modern anthropology for understanding that may contribute to the kind of internationalism we want to achieve.

Despite the conflict and turbulence of our time, there are indications of "one world" in prospect. The growing economic interdependence of peoples, the achievement of a global communications system and a global transportation system, the internationalization of science and many humanities – all are signs. In terms of political organization, we had the League of Nations (which we rate a failure despite its many achievements), and we now have the United Nations, with its limitations. Whatever their defects, both organizations express human hope and effort for peace and a secure and better life for mankind. Special agencies and programs of the UN, like UNICEF (UN Children's Fund), UNESCO (UN Educational, Scientific, and Cultural Organization), or WHO (World

This paper is an edited version of "Anthropology and the coming internationalism," a lecture Alexander Lesser delivered at the University of Calgary, Alberta, Canada, on October 8, 1974. It is published here for the first time by permission of the Department of Anthropology, the University of Calgary.

Health Organization), may have contributed more consistently to sustain the hope than the Security Council or the General Assembly.

Recently, ecological realizations of the finite limitations of our planet, and the imperative need for *global* planning in the use of world resources to meet human needs, are awakening many people to the urgency of a more mature internationalism. Without it, increasing pollution, exhaustion of resources, increasing populations, and war threaten human extinction.

The signs of internationalism, or internationalization, to which I have referred do not involve a new or recent kind of human relationship. They are instead a stage of evolution of the interdependence and interaction of human groups, an interdependence which existed in early primitive life and has been developing in extent and in intensity throughout human history. Though limited by rudimentary technology, a primitive human group – except in rare instances – was nonetheless part of a network of interdependent and interactive relations with other groups; and such networks served a wide range of functions. In primitive Australia, for example, networks included in social relationships, often intermarriage and blood brotherhood; in religion, often shared rituals and ceremonies, especially initiation ceremonies; in political and legal structures, both feud and truce-making, safe-conduct, blood-brotherhood, and widely extended kinship ties; and in economic relations, barter or gift-exchange forms of trade, with reciprocal benefits, which overcame restrictions of limited local resources and made resources at a distance locally available. Such trade was not impersonal – the kind we are accustomed to – but personalized, usually involving friendships and blood-brotherhood.

Early networks, however, were limited in their extent. Technological inventions increased their range. The domestication of animals in the Neolithic made transportation at greater distances possible, as did the improvement of ships with sails. The compass made sea-going shipping possible. From the 1400s on, the demands of mercantile trade stimulated what – from a European standpoint – we call the era of exploration and discovery. It continued until all continents and most peoples were known to Europeans.

But for thousands of years mankind did not become aware of itself as the population of a small and limited planet. The industrial revolution, economic in motivation and technological in means, continued the expansion and intensification of global networks. It is only very recently in the history of the industrialized world that the realization of our global limitations and problems has come about. Our political structures were not designed to deal with these limitations. Rather they are the outcome of past history. Primitive political structures were based on kinship. In a kin-structured group, members tend to be the children of members; descent defines citizenship. There is a tendency toward homogeneity of language, and of values and ways of life. Men (but not groups) may fight, and fights may lead to feuds, but such societies are not structured for war. They may fight for personal reasons, but they do not fight for conquest and booty.

Trade is probably the key to understanding those fundamental changes which ended the kinship age. Trade meant increased demands for local products to be exchanged or exported. Increased production of local products, and increased dependence upon imports for other products resulted in local specialization in production, and, for a region of intertrading specializers, in a division of labor in the overall society of the region.

Under conditions of a division of labor, the roles and relationships of people are specialized and economically determined. Even merchants, and traveling merchants, can appear. Local areas as trade areas, as areas for obtaining specialized products, become basic. Production for external trade geared to land, rather than production for a consuming population, then begins to lead to what are territorially defined political structures. Through a complex historical evolution such structures become the State or Nation.

In the territorially based group or state, place of birth defines citizenship or membership. The tendency is toward diversity of languages and values and ways of life, especially as older regions, with their historically developed divisions of labor, become regional political units. Ethnic groups *within* the political state or nation, and/or minorities, are born.

The bounded territories which define the state, and the trade routes and trade relations fundamental to their economic and political existence, require for their maintenance organized military structures and action by the state, namely, war. Trade and territory are thus the two great causes of the invention and practice of war.

It is the nation-state, this form which continues into the present to be our principal political structure, that is considered by many to be the great political achievement of man. From its territorial base, the nation-state takes its doctrine of sovereignty, and from its wars and conquests its rights to maintain military power and to make war. Such a development, and the ways in which it is conventionally regarded, lead me here to reminiscence.

When I was in college, after World War I, it seems to me now that we accepted two quite contradictory ideas as belonging together. From the nineteenth century and through the First World War, we understood the development of nations, especially in Europe, as political progress – progress toward the unification of peoples and, we hoped, toward democractic governments. Together with that view, we accepted the right of nations to sovereignty, nationalism (even chauvinistic nationalism), military power, and the right to use such power in war. Yet at the same time, we saw both national unification and the internationalism of the time – as expressed in the League of Nations – as aimed at an end to war and toward an international network of peoples organized for peace.

But these two ideas are antithetical, as we discover increasingly in the conflicting nationalisms of the present. Sovereign nations, militarized, with war as an accepted instrument of their action, may talk peace and even make written agreements for peace, but they do not mesh in peace, because they are structured for war. The weakness and what we call the failure of the UN to be what its founders dreamed they were creating is in the fact of its actual organization of member-nations.

The European conquest of the non-European world gave us increasing and, over time, vast knowledge of non-European peoples and culture – the foundation materials of anthropological studies. But that same conquest also gave Europeans convictions and ideas that modern anthropology shows are erroneous. Indigenous peoples, wherever European power reached, were engulfed by European settlement, or structured as colonies for exploitation. The supremacy of conquest meant to the European mind innate European superiority and cultural preeminence, the intrinsic right to master and enslave others, bolstered by dogmas or racism. And it meant also that European institutions, like the nation-state with its sovereign rights, was the apex of human political evolutionary achievement.

Yet comparative study of the variations in the ways of life of the many peoples of the world has made the smug ethnocentricity of Europeans doubtful. Human culture varied; human institutions varied. They were not everywhere the same. Yet the diversity found everywhere was human. One by one, assumptions about universals of human behavior, which were supposed to flow from innate human instincts, had to be discarded, as our knowledge of various cultures revealed immense variety, and contradictory forms of belief and behavior.

Objective comparative studies of human groups, culminating in the anthropological concept and theory of human culture, provided the most convincing alternative to pre-scientific assumptions about humanity. The structured human behavior of any time and place, of any human community, was a product of time and history, just as was that of Europeans. The ways of life of any people were rooted in the human capacity for learning – learning and relearning that takes place in each generation, from parents and other predecessors – and were not predetermined by instincts or biological predispositions. Over time, all human cultures are linked in a continuity going back to cultural beginnings.

This broad theory of human culture offers for the history of human ways of life, as the theory of evolution provides for the history of all biological forms, a framework for understanding. Analogous to Darwin's basic idea of evolution in biological forms as *descent with modification*, the theory of culture offers in the historical evolution of cultures the conception of *continuity with diversification*.

Such anthropological perspective requires a critical review of ideas which, though erroneous, are still so firmly held that they limit our view of the possibilities for a humane and peaceful world. I have in mind here racist ideas, evaluations of cultural or civilizational systems as better or worse, and faith in the finality of the political nation and political nationalism, with its sovereignty and militaristic rights to make war and its confident claim to make all people under its jurisdiction uniform in their culture and in their allegiance to the nation-state.

Race, and the racist prejudices and antagonisms that go with it, need only brief comment. Biologically, as a question of taxonomy or classification of mankind into natural subdivisions, race is being rapidly discarded in anthropology as a relatively useless concept, in favor of recognition that there is one *human race*. Biological variations do not cluster in neat packages, and there are no proofs of built-in inequalities or inferiorities of peoples that could prevent their effective participation in modern life, including our industrial civilization. The whole race episode in our history, looking backward, can be understood as an expression of the dominance of nations and empires and their subordination of others to exploitation for national or imperial ends.

The idea of superior and inferior cultures and/or civilizations persists as an offshoot of the idea of progress which dominated Western thinking during so much of the eighteenth and nineteenth centuries. The idea of progress was inherent in the conception that evolution was orthogenetic – unilinear, directed, following one predetermined course. According to the orthogenetic conception of evolution, every culture was at some step or stage and, as such, has achieved progress and a degree of superiority beyond certain others, but was at a lower level of achievement than those which had surpassed it. The exceptions were the culture at the highest level of progress and achievement – usually one's own – and that culture which represented the lowest level, usually some technologically simple, primitive people.

This conviction that we can assess and evaluate other peoples' ways (usually to their detriment) has been weakened by more mature understanding of each culture on its own terms; but most of us still labor under the idea that "progress" is necessary, and that change must lead ever onward and upward. That the standards used in evaluation, and the idea of progress itself, are culture-based and culture-bound is a recognition slow in coming. Alternatively, we have begun to learn that a commitment to *stability* and to continued maintenance of achieved and cherished values, however different – a commitment once especially characteristic of the Orient – is as much a cultural achievement, to be respected on its own terms. Evaluating different ways of human life in order to elevate some and to derogate others reflects an ethnocentricity that must eventually give way to cultural and civilizational maturity.

Finally, the tendency to treat the nation-state with its territorial sovereignty as a sacrosanct political achievement which must be preserved at any cost has also become subject to historical understanding. The nation-state itself and the reverential attitudes toward it are also cultural-historical developments. Like any other cultural institution, no matter how revered, the nation as political structure is man-made; it is neither natural, nor inevitable, nor unchangeable. In erecting international structures, we need not forever assume that the nation is an irreplaceable, unmodifiable building-block. If other administrative structures are required for global peace and security, there is nothing in nature or in culture or in man which prevents their creation.

War, that ultimate sanction of the nation in action, is a man-made institution, like the nation structure which practices it. The nation or state, with its centralized power and its economic drive for expansion by conquest, developed war – and still goes on developing it – in order to promote the nation and national interests. It is not in the interest of global mankind that wars are fought.

War is not a fact of nature or of human nature; it is not found in all human cultures or societies. War can be changed, or eliminated, like any other political or cultural institution, by human planning or action. Institutions or structures of peace, those which exist, are as man-made as are those of war; they can be expanded or built, if men want them, by human planning and human action.

Perhaps most critical for the resolution of present international problems is the philosophy and practice of assimilation, a philosophy invested by the nation to affirm its rights to make all those under its power and jurisdiction uniform in culture with its dominant group and committed to allegiance to the nation-state.

Assimilation became the dominant practice of the nation in dealing with ethnic aliens who were engulfed, conquered, or taken in by immigration. In theory, ethnic differences could not coexist within the country without conflict, and assimilation assured that all would be patriotic citizens, available for military action in national armies fighting for national interests. Education has been fundamentally influenced by this conception. In virtually all nations, education is essentially an attempt at assimilation, with curriculums overweighted to develop national uniformity and chauvinistic patriotism.

As yet, confidence in the theory and practice of assimilation has only begun to be affected by evidence that it has been a failure almost everywhere. Ethnic differences – in traditions, in religions, and in other ways – can and do coexist within countries without conflict.

In assimilation, individuals may give up their heritage and accept the culture of an adopted land; but ethnic or cultural groups usually show a tenacity to persist. In fact, ethnic identity and its demands (especially when frustrated) have become an outstanding feature of conflict situations in virtually all ethnically heterogeneous political nations.

Illustrations are many and varied. Indigenous populations engulfed by European expansions resist assimilation. In the United States, for example, surviving American Indian groups, after two hundred years of genocide or forced assimilation, stubbornly persist in maintaining American Indian identity. They pose the fundamental question of "the right not to assimilate." Australia has similar problems with surviving Australian aboriginals and indigenous populations in parts of Melanesia.

Human mobility, by migration and immigration has made countries ethnically heterogeneous, and assimilation has not been able to make the heterogeneity go away. In the United States, for example, the effort from the beginning to Anglo-Saxonize non-English European immigrants has left the country with viable ethnic minority groups of virtually every nationality and language that came. Recent movements to the United States have merely enlarged and further complicated that heterogeneity. There are also recent and long-standing cases of failure of countries to impose unified identity upon populations diverse in traditions and ethnicity. Recently, for example, as independence came, African countries were organized by making "nations" of the bounded areas administered colonially as units, wholly disregarding the tribal diversities such units included. Conflicts in the Congo, East Africa, Nigeria, and elsewhere ensued. When India became an independent nation, Pakistan withdrew from it; then Bangladesh asserted its freedom from Pakistan. There are many ethnic groups, like the Naga peoples of Northeast India, still demanding autonomy.

Older situations await resolution, despite generations of attempted unification by assimilation: the Basques of Spain and France; the Catalans of Spain – let us recall how Pablo Casals, presenting his *Ode to the United*

Nations a few years ago, declared himself a Catalonian, not a Spaniard. Belgium is torn by language and cultural differences between the Flemish and the French (the Walloons). The Czechs and Slovaks of Czechoslovakia, and the Serbs, Croats, and Slovenes of Yugoslavia have not developed national political unity. In Russia, absorbed nationalities, like the Ukrainians, or the Latvians, Estonians, and Lithuanians, and others, demand a degree of freedom and autonomy that disputes the Russian claim to national unity. In Canada, the question of Quebec and English Canada continues unresolved.

The long-standing assumption about European history that the formation of nations, unifying diverse peoples, was a mark of progress is open to question. It was usually a victory of force and domination by particular ethnic elements in power, and few consider Germany or Italy, for example, to have been ethnically integrated. More striking is the United Kingdom, perhaps the earliest such "unification." Wales was united with England in 1536, Scotland in 1707, yet nationalist movements for autonomy are strong today in both. In Wales it involves a strong revival of Welsh language. In Scotland, the Scottish Nationalist Party, asking for an independent Scotland, is a force in elections.

Ethnic identity or nationality are not wiped out, in such cases, by the superimposition of alien political power. To a people with a tradition, a language, a culture, and historical memories reaching back in time, freedom means autonomous freedom, freedom to live their own way. Second class citizenship, which subordinates and denies their rights to be themselves, is usually at best a transient status, resisted and overcome whenever possible.

It is time we learned that assimilation is not an answer to conditions of ethnic diversity. Realism requires an alternative. In the United States near the turn of the century, the effort to reduce diverse peoples to a uniform stew in some assimilative melting pot was not only recognized as a failure, but the failure was heralded by some who saw its future human implications of an alternative. Randolph Bourne, in his *History of a Literary Radical*, acknowledges the meaning of cultural pluralism:

The failure of the melting pot, far from closing the great American democratic experiment, means that it has only just begun. Whatever American Nationalism turns out to be, we see already that it will have a color richer and more exciting than our ideal has hitherto encompassed. In a world which has dreamed of internationalism, we find we have all unawares been building up the first international nation. The voices which have cried for a tight and jealous nationalism of the European pattern are failing. From that ideal, however valiantly and disinterestedly it has been set for us, time and tendency have moved us further and further away. What we have achieved has been rather a cosmopolitan federation of national colonies, of foreign cultures, from which the sting of devastating competition has been removed. America is already the world-federation in miniature, the continent where for the first time in history has been achieved the miracle of hope, the peaceful living side by side, with character substantially preserved, of the most heterogeneous peoples under the sun. Here, notwithstanding our tragic failures of adjustment, the outlines are already too clear not to give us a new vision and a new orientation of the American mind in the world (Bourne 1956:276–7 [first published 1920]).

Bourne may have been overoptimistic; but his grasp of realities was profound. If, within a country, assimilation is not a realistic answer to questions of ethnic diversity, some form of cultural pluralism is inescapable. Moreover, even if a high degree of uniformity could be created within a country, how – without prohibiting immigration – could it be maintained for even a year?

There is also the more profound question of whether ethnic uniformity – usually assumed to be an end to be sought – is desirable. Many would affirm that the diversity eliminated is to be preferred to the sameness achieved. Assimilation is ordinarily treated as a policy within countries. If, by eliminating ethnic differences, conflicts could be avoided, does this apply to the diversity of countries as well? Countries differ in their traditions, languages, religions, ethical value systems, social life, political and economic systems, and in many other ways. Does the philosophy of assimilation suggest, for example, that Chinese or Russian will disappear in the foreseeable future, in favor of English? Or that Christianity, or Buddhism, or Mohammedanism, will give way to one another? Clearly, on a world basis, the impossibility of assimilation as a procedure is obvious. Ethnic differences in the world, as well as within many countries, are here to stay. Cultural pluralism is inevitable for the world at large.

These considerations are, I think, vital to internationalism. At present, our efforts to create it are too exclusively founded on political considerations. If we are to achieve global peace and security in a world rich in ethnic diversity, the cultural realities of mankind, and the rights and claims of human groups to their own identity, must be realized. In a world at peace, without national sovereignties and military organizations, global administration can be structured to accept cultural pluralism and ethnic identities and to make their carriers free.

We know the human potential for change, for self-directed change toward desired ends, is unlimited by anything in nature. Human culture may itself interfere with the cultural changes and development men want, but it cannot do so indefinitely. The internationalism which increases and intensifies interdependence and the interrelation of peoples can also make global structures and the linking pathways needed by mankind. To do so, that internationalism must be pluralistic in design to reflect and safeguard thereby the human diversity treasured by each people for itself, and essential to mankind for all peoples.

If we ask fundamental questions about man and his attainment of global peace, security, and a good life, we must take a long view. The ideal ends we may want to achieve seem blocked now and in the short run by formidable obstacles – by chauvinistic nationalism, by war, and by deeply embedded racism. Yet the realities of history are that these are *human* institutions and institutional attitudes. If they are made by humans, then as such they can be changed by humans, in the interests of all humankind.

Notes

Editor's Note: Many of what were footnoted items, particularly references to specific authors and works (e.g., "Boas 1898") are now in the text. Notes merely explaining that a particular article had first been delivered as a paper at a scholarly meeting have often been reworded, but all substantive footnotes have been retained as in the original articles. Explanatory notes that I have added have been marked with an asterisk. Lesser was a meticulous scholar, but in a few instances his references were incomplete or faulty; such instances have been noted.

1. This paper, with some variations in content, was presented as a lecture in 1973 at the University of Pennsylvania and Yale University, in 1974 at Calgary University and Cornell University, and in 1975 at Barnard College, Hofstra University, McMaster University, and the Johns Hopkins University. The author acknowledges the kindness of the American Philosophical Society for use of materials from the Boas collection.

2. Dr. Marian W. Smith was trained at Columbia and was an active anthropologist for years in the United States before she went abroad, where later she became Secretary of the Royal Anthropological Institute of Great Britain and Ireland. She was well experienced in both American anthropology and British social anthropology.

3. All quotations in this paragraph are from Boas's Diary from Baffinland (APS, 2).

4. This quotation is from "Proceedings of the American Ethnological Society" in the *American Anthropologist* 23 (1921):514.

*5. The references are inaccurate, and I have not been able to locate the sources of these quotations.

*6. This passage is taken from Malinowski 1929, but Lesser changed the wording slightly.

*7. Lesser is referring here to a now famous statement by Lowie: "Nor are the facts of culture history without bearing on the adjustment of our own future. To that planless hodge-podge, that thing of shreds and patches called civilization, its historian can no longer yield superstitious reverence" (Lowie 1920:441).

*8. A reference to Kroeber's use of statistics to hypothesize differential degrees of historical connection between different societies. "To order and classify, Kroeber relied heavily upon counting, that is, on statistics" (Wolf 1981:51). Wolf's discussion of Kroeber's method is useful. See also Beals 1968:458.

*9. Garrick Mallery (1831–94), American folklorist and anthropologist, was especially well known for his work on American Indian gestures and sign-languages. A routine search of the early volumes of the *Journal of Folklore* failed to turn up the papers to which Lesser refers. William Sturtevant has suggested that the papers may have been written by a different author, and Lesser confused two names, but I have not pursued this possibility further.

*10. Lesser's mention of White is of interest. Few American anthropologists were as hostile to Boas as White (cf. White 1949, passim), and White's determinism probably had limited appeal to Lesser. But White was consistently evolutionary in his outlook.

11. A general view implicit in Sumner's (1906) influential *Folkways*. Wirth (1938:2) remarks that Sumner pictures a primitive society "as small isolated groups of human beings scattered over a vast territory."

12. Honigmann distinguishes "community" and "society," using a field concept for the latter.

13. I have also commented on this in Lesser 1959.

14. The census shows a marked increase in Indians during recent generations and a rate of population growth more rapid than that of the country as a whole or of any other identifiable group. There are now [1961] between 400,000 and 500,000 Indians in the continental United States and Alaska. And, if the present rate of increase continues, descendants of the original inhabitants may be as numerous in another generation as their ancestors were in Columbus's day.

15. By 1924, more than two-thirds of the Indians were citizens under treaties and agreements. In that year citizenship was confirmed by enactment for all Indians born in the country. Indians have full rights of citizenship, which include, of course, the right to complete freedom of movement anywhere. The time is past when Indian communities can be dismissed as "segregation" or as "concentration camps."

16. However, Indians pay all other taxes paid by other citizens, including real estate taxes on Indian-owned land not in trust status.

*17. Felix S. Cohen (1907–53), lawyer, chief of the Indian Land Survey, United States Department of Justice, was author of the *Handbook of Federal Indian Law* (1942, Washington, D.C.: Government Printing Office).

18. The act was in force forty-seven years. During the period, two-thirds of Indian-owned lands of 1887 were alienated from Indian ownership, principally as a result of the procedure of first individualizing land holdings and then removing them from trust status. Some tribes were not subject to allotment, especially tribes in the Southwest. Of the many who were subject to the program but opposed it, few wholly escaped; the Red Lake Chippewas of Minnesota are perhaps the outstanding case. Some of the disastrous effects of the allotment program were remedied in the Indian New Deal period that began in 1934. In 1960, one tribe, the northern Cheyennes of Montana, was trying to promote a tribal "Fifty-Year Unallotment Program" to return all allotted lands still Indian-owned to tribal ownership.

*19. See note 17.

20. The Bear Dance of recent years among the Pawnee, such as that which James Murie studied and recorded, was a Ghost Dance revival. The following quotations from Murie's account in *Ceremonies of the Pawnee*, in press, Bureau of Ethnology [see note 21], serve to illustrate the account given above of these revivals. The account is presented by Murie as of the Skiri Bear Dance, but I have found on internal evidence, such as the affiliation of the owners of the revived ceremony, the choice of individuals for the leaderships, the story or teaching associated with the ceremony, the fact that the bears are "yellow bears," etc., that the form must be considered that of the Pitahawirat band.

> At the death of Bear Chief of the Pitahawirat, the main bearskin and other things belonging to the Bear Society were buried with him. He had not taught the secret ceremony to anyone; so it was supposed that the Bear Society was lost. At a meeting of the medicine society when the ceremony had ended, a woman arose, her name Woman Yellow Corn, and said, "I had a visitor. I saw Bear Chief wearing the bear robe over his shoulders and the bear-claw neckpiece around his neck. He was painted with yellow earthen clay, and had black streaks from each eye down the face. He said, 'My sister, Father (bear) and Mother (cedar-tree) have not had any smoke for many years. We (dead people) are watching for our people to have the ceremony. The people think the ceremony is lost. It is not, for one of the Bear men who knows the ceremony is still with you. I ask that you tell the

people so that they can have the ceremony, for it is time.' I woke up and the last few days have been crying to think that I should be the one to tell you. I have a cow which you can have so you can have the ceremony." Then she began to cry.

The leaders of the Bear ceremony each in their turn arose, went to the woman and blessed her. . . . They said, "My sister, this is very hard. None of us know the ceremony but Father (bear) and Mother (cedar-tree) will plan a way themselves so we can have the ceremony. . . ."

Some days later the members of the Bear Society met and compared their knowledge of the ceremony. When all had spoken a man named Big Star . . . questioned the others as to their knowledge of the ceremony. He found that none in the meeting knew the ceremony. So he said, "Brothers, this is hard. You see I am paralyzed, and I could not sit and carry the ceremony out. If you will all agree I will try it. Before we do anything we must select men to be the leaders. You and I know that there are some men here who are descendants of deceased men who were leaders in the Bear Society. . . ." So he selected . . . Little Warchief, . . . Little Sun, . . . Good Buffalo, . . . and Roaming Chief. . . .

[These men were ceremonially inducted into office. Big Star then seated himself with these leaders at the altar and made arrangements to collect among the people the ceremonial utensils, etc., for a set of things needed to carry out the ceremony.]

When all the others had gone out, Big Star told the four men to watch as he carried on the ceremony, that he would carry on the ceremony for them. He also told that Tirawahat had planned through the woman for them to have the ceremony, so he was willing to carry the ceremony on for them without pay; that in olden times men paid to learn the going after the Mother Cedar-Tree; that he himself did not purchase the right to carry the ceremony on, but that Bear Chief, who was the last man to know the ceremony, had given him the right to sit near him and watch; that Bear Chief took pity on him and taught him the ceremony and songs without pay. He then told them to go to their homes, that on the morrow when they entered the lodge each one was to take his seat. They were then dismissed with the exception of Little Warchief.

When they were alone Big Star questioned Little Warchief about the songs and asked if he knew them. Little Warchief said, "Yes, I know the songs." Big Star was glad of this for although he could carry on the ceremony, he was afraid that he would not be able to sing the cedar-tree songs.

[Later at the preliminary feast to set the date of the ceremony,] when all were in, Big Star said, "You, who are sitting at the altar and those of you at the stations, old men and chiefs. Today we sit in this lodge as men of the Bear Society. We are gathered together here, through Woman Yellow Corn, who had a vision of one of our departed relatives who asked that we have this ceremony, that Father and Mother might receive our smoke. . . ."

Inasmuch as Murie, in reporting this and the rest of his account, was unaware of the nature of this whole procedure as a revival, it is interesting substantiation and illustration of the interpretation I have outlined above. Murie's confusion about the band affiliation of the ceremony is no doubt due to the pooling of knowledge, which does include men of various bands. Of interest is that in the account of Murie of the felling of the cedar tree, the tree is made to fall westward, a Ghost Dance orientation; in earlier times the tree would have had to fall eastward. The whole nature of this revival of a ceremony whose owner is dead, and whose bundle is buried in the ground, would have been impossible without the Ghost Dance and its doctrines.

*21. Murie's *Ceremonies of the Pawnee* was not published until 1981. Skillfully edited and integrated by Douglas Parks, it provides an extraordinarily rich account of the ceremonial life of both the Skiri and South bands of the Pawnee. Parks mentions Lesser among those who assisted him with the preparation of the work. The material provided by Lesser, which he summarizes here in note 20, appears in the section entitled "The Bear Dance of the Pitahawirata," in vol. 2, pp. 319ff.

References

All of the works Lesser cited in his articles are listed here, as are those I have referred to in the introductory materials. The articles reprinted in this volume have not been included here; for full references see the note on the first page of each chapter.

American Anthropological Association
1943   *Franz Boas: 1858–1942*. Memoir No. 61. Menasha, Wis.: American Anthropological Association.
APS (American Philosophical Society, Boas Archives), Philadelphia.
    1. Vita. Ms. post-Gymnasium.
    2. Diary from Baffinland.
    3. Letter to Ernst Boas, August 16, 1914.
    4. Letter from Max Yergan to Helene Boas Yampolsky.
Arensberg, Conrad, and Solon T. Kimball
1940   *Family and Community in Ireland*. Cambridge, Mass.: Harvard University Press.
Barnes, John A.
1954   Classes and committees in a Norwegian island parish. *Human Relations* 7:39–58.
Beals, Ralph
1968   Alfred L. Kroeber. In *International Encyclopedia of the Social Sciences* 8:454–63.
Benedict, Ruth
1936   *Patterns of Culture*. Boston: Houghton and Mifflin.
Boas, Franz
1884   *The Central Eskimo*. Sixth Annual Report of the Bureau of American Ethnology (1884–5). Washington, D.C.: Government Printing Office.
1897   *The Social Organization and the Secret Societies of the Kwakiutl Indians*. Report of the U.S. National Museum for 1895, 311–738.
1899   The cephalic index. *American Anthropologist* 1:448–61.
1901   *Kathlamet Texts*. Smithsonian Institution, Bureau of American Ethnology Bulletin No. 26. Washington, D.C.: Government Printing Office.
1907   Response to address by the President of Columbia University. *American Anthropologist* 9:646–7.
1910   The real race problem. *Crisis* 1:22–5.

1911a   *Changes in Bodily Form of Descendants of Immigrants*. Senate Document 208, 61st Congress, Second Session. Washington, D.C.. Government Printing Office. (Reprinted 1912 by Columbia University Press, New York.)

1911b   *The Mind of Primitive Man*. New York: Macmillan.

1927   *Primitive Art*. Oslo: Aschehoug.

1928   *Anthropology and Modern Life*. New York: Norton.

1930a   Anthropology. In *Encyclopedia of the Social Sciences* 2:73–110.

1930b   *The Religion of the Kwakiutl Indians*. Columbia University Contributions to Anthropology X. New York: Columbia University Press.

1938a   An anthropologist's credo. *The Nation* 147:201–4.

1938b   Introduction. In Franz Boas, ed., *General Anthropology*, 1–6. Boston: Heath.

1940a   *Race, Language and Culture*. New York: Macmillan.

1940b   The genetic basis for democracy. *Science Bookshelf* 1:3–4, 24, 26. From a speech at a panel discussion on race and race prejudice at the New York World's Fair, October 14, 1939.

1945   *Race and Democratic Society*. New York: Augustin.

Bourne, Randolph
1956   *History of a Literary Radical*. New York: Russell. (First published 1920.)

Childe, V. Gordon
1936   *Man Makes Himself*. London: Watts.

1946   *What Happened in History*. New York: Penguin Books.

1951   *Social Evolution*. London: Watts.

Codere, Helen
1966   Introduction. In Franz Boas, *Kwakiutl Ethnography*. Chicago: University of Chicago Press.

Dewey, John
1932   Human nature. In *Encyclopedia of the Social Sciences* 7:531–6.

Durkheim, Emile
1915   *Elementary Forms of the Religious Life*. Cited in Honigmann 1959.

Firth, Raymond
1951   *Elements of Social Organization*. London: Watts.

Fortes, Meyer
1949   *The Web of Kinship Among the Tallensi*. Oxford: Oxford University Press.

Fortune, Reo F.
1932   *The Sorcerors of Dobu*. London: Routledge and Sons.

Fried, Morton, Marvin Harris, and Robert Murphy, eds.
1968   *War: The Anthropology of Armed Aggression*. Garden City, N.Y.: Natural History Press.

Gluckman, Max
1949   *Malinowski's Sociological Theories*. Rhodes-Livingstone Papers No. 16, Oxford.

Goldenweiser, Alexander
1937   *Anthropology*. New York: Crofts.

Goldman, Irving
1941   The Alkatcho Carrier: Historical background of crest prerogatives. *American Anthropologist* 43:396–418.
Goldschmidt, Walter, ed.
1959   *The Anthropology of Franz Boas*. American Anthropological Association Memoir No. 89, vol. 61, no. 5, pt. 2. Menasha, Wis.: American Anthropological Association.
Hobhouse, L. T., G. C. Wheeler, and M. Ginsberg
1915   *The Material Culture and Social Institutions of the Simpler Peoples: An Essay in Correlation*. London: Chapman & Hall.
Honigmann, John
1959   *The World of Man*. New York: Harper.
Hunt, G. T.
1940   *The Wars of the Iroquois*. Madison: University of Wisconsin Press.
Hyde, G. E.
1959   *Indians of the High Plains*. Norman: University of Oklahoma Press.
Keur, John Y., and Dorothy L. Keur
1955   *The Deeply Rooted*. Assen, The Netherlands: Royal Van Gorcum.
Kroeber, Alfred L.
1935   History and science in anthropology. *American Anthropologist* 37:539–69.
1943   Franz Boas: The man. In American Anthropological Association 1943:5–26.
1948   *Anthropology*. New York: Harcourt Brace.
1959   Preface. In Goldschmidt 1959:v–vii.
LaBarre, Weston
1970   *The Ghost Dance: The Origins of Religion*. New York: Dell (Delta Books).
Lesser, Alexander
1929a   Kinship origins in the light of some distributions. *American Anthropologist* 31:710–30.
1929b   Siouan kinship. Ph.D. dissertation, Columbia University, New York.
1959   Some comments on the concept of the intermediate society. In *Proceedings of the 1959 Annual Spring Meeting of the American Ethnological Society*, 11–13. Seattle: University of Washington.
1968a   Franz Boas. In *International Encyclopedia of the Social Sciences* 2:99–110.
1968b   War and the state. In Fried et al. 1968:92–6.
1977   Commentary on "Functionalism in social anthropology" and "Social fields and the evolution of society." Unpublished transcript of tape recording of lecture given at Columbia University, New York, in 1977, 23 pp.
1978   *The Pawnee Ghost Dance Hand Game: Ghost Dance Revival and Ethnic Identity*. Madison: University of Wisconsin Press. (Originally published 1933 by Columbia University Press, New York, as Vol. XVI in Columbia University Contributions to Anthropology).

1979   Caddoan kinship systems. *Nebraska History* 60:260–71.
Lowie, Robert H.
1920   *Primitive Society*. New York: Boni & Liveright.
1944a   Franz Boas: 1858–1942. *Journal of American Folklore* 57:59–64.
1944b   *History of Ethnological Theory*. New York: Rinehart.
Lynd, Robert S., and Helen M. Lynd
1929   *Middletown*. New York: Harcourt Brace.
Maine, Henry J. S.
1861   *Ancient Law*. London: Murray
1871   *Village Communities East and West*. London: Murray.
Malinowski, Bronislaw
1922   *Argonauts of the Western Pacific*. Studies in Economic and Political Science, London School of Economics Monograph 65. London.
1926   *Myth and Primitive Psychology*. London: Norton.
1929   Social anthropology. In *Encyclopedia Britannica*, 14th ed., vol. 20:863–70.
1944   *A Scientific Theory of Culture*. Chapel Hill: University of North Carolina Press.
Merton, Robert K., Leonard Broom, and Leonard Cottrell, eds.
1959   *Sociology Today*. New York: Basic Books.
Mintz, Sidney W.
1981   Ruth Benedict. In Silverman 1981:142–61.
Mintz, Sidney W., and Richard Price
1976   *An Anthropological Approach to the Afro-American Past: A Caribbean Perspective*. Ishi Occasional Papers in Social Change 2. Philadelphia: Ishi.
Mooney, James
1896   *The Ghost-Dance Religion*. Fourteenth Annual Report of the Bureau of American Ethnology (1892–3), pt. 1. Washington, D.C.: Government Printing Office.
Morgan, Lewis Henry
1877   *Ancient Society*. New York: Holt.
Murie, James R.
1981   *Ceremonies of the Pawnee*. Edited by Douglas Parks. 2 vols. Smithsonian Contributions to Ethnology 27. Washington, D.C.: Smithsonian Institution Press.
Oakley, Kenneth P.
1959   *Man the Tool-Maker*. Chicago: University of Chicago Press.
Parks, Douglas, ed. 1981. See Murie.
Radcliffe-Brown, A.R.
1935   On the concept of function in social science. *American Anthropologist* 37:394–402. (Reprinted 1952 in A. R. Radcliffe-Brown, *Structure and Function in Primitive Society*, 178–87. Glencoe, Ill.: Free Press.)
Redfield, Robert
1941   *The Folk Culture of Yucatan*. Chicago: University of Chicago Press.
1947   The folk society. *American Journal of Sociology* 52:293–308.

158   References

1953   *The Primitive World and Its Transformations*. Ithaca, N. Y.: Cornell University Press.

1955   *The Little Community*. Chicago: University of Chicago Press.

1956   *Peasant Society and Culture*. Chicago: University of Chicago Press.

Rees, Alwyn

1950   *Life in a Welsh Countryside*. Cardiff: University of Wales.

Rivers, William H. R.

1914   *Kinship and Social Organization*. London: Constable.

Schapera, I.

1930   *The Khoisan Peoples of South Africa*. London: Routledge and Sons.

Schifter, Richard

1970   Trends in federal Indian administration. *South Dakota Law Review* 15:1–21.

Schumpeter, Joseph

1955   *Social Classes; Imperialism*. New York: New American Library (Meridian Books).

Silverman, Sydel, ed.

1981   *Totems and Teachers*. New York: Columbia University Press.

Simpson, George G.

1950   *The Meaning of Evolution*. New Haven: Yale University Press.

Sjoberg, Gideon

1959   Comparative urban sociology. In Merton et al. 1959:334–59.

Smith, Marian W.

1959   Boas' "natural history" approach to field method. In Goldschmidt 1959:46–60.

Steward, Julian H.

1949   Cultural causality and law: a trial formulation of the development of early civilizations. *American Anthropologist* 51:1–27.

Stocking, George W., Jr.

1968   *Race, Culture and Evolution: Essays in the History of Anthropology*. New York: Free Press.

1974   *The Shaping of American Anthropology, 1883–1911: A Franz Boas Reader*. New York: Basic Books.

Strong, [William] Duncan

1936   Review of *The Pawnee Ghost Dance Hand Game*. *American Anthropologist* 38:112–13.

Sumner, William G.

1906   *Folkways*. Boston: Ginn.

Tyler, Stephen A., ed.

1969   *Concepts and Assumptions in Contemporary Anthropology*. Proceedings of the Southern Anthropological Society 3. Athens: University of Georgia Press.

Tyler, Edward B.

1889   On a method of investigating the development of institutions: applied to laws of marriage and descent. *Journal of the Anthropological Institute* 17:245–72.

Wallace, Anthony F. C.
1965   *The Ghost-Dance Religion and the Sioux Outbreak of 1890.* Chicago: University of Chicago Press.
Washburn, Sherwood L.
1963   The study of race. *American Anthropologist* 65:521–32.
Wheeler, Gerald C.
1910   *The Tribe and Intertribal Relations in Australia.* London: Murray.
White, Leslie A.
1943   Energy and the evolution of culture. *American Anthropologist* 45:335–56.
1949   *The Science of Culture.* New York: Farrar, Straus & Giroux.
Williams, W. M.
1956   *Gosforth: The Sociology of an English Village.* London: Routledge and Kegan Paul.
Wilson, Edmund
1960   *Apologies to the Iroquois.* New York: Farrar, Straus & Cudahy.
Wirth, Louis
1938   Urbanism as a way of life. *American Journal of Sociology* 44:1–24.
Wolf, Eric R.
1969   American anthropologists and American society. In Tyler 1969:3–11.
1981   Alfred L. Kroeber. In Silverman 1981:36–55.
1982   *Europe and the People Without History.* Berkeley: University of California Press.

Index